HOW TO WRITE
FOR TEENAGERS

Other Allison & Busby 'Writers' Guides'

HOW TO WRITE FOR TEENAGERS

David Silwyn Williams

Allison & Busby
Published by W. H. Allen & Co. Plc

An Allison & Busby book
Published in 1989 by
W. H. Allen & Co. Plc
Sekforde House
175/9 St John Street
London EC1V 4LL

Phototypeset by Input Typesetting Ltd., London
Printed in Great Britain
by Cox & Wyman Ltd, Reading, Berkshire

ISBN 0 7490 0015 5

CONTENTS

1

INTRODUCTION

So you'd like to write for teenagers – novels as well as short stories.

Good.

I say good because writing short stories and novels for teenagers is an expanding market for writers – and the rewards can be substantial, especially if your publisher or agent sells your work abroad either in English to various countries in the Commonwealth, or negotiates the sale of translation rights to other European countries. When that happens, your royalties can be doubled. So what are you waiting for?

Though some magazines have folded in the last few years, new ones are constantly taking their place. A quick glance along the shelves of your local newsagent will show you the range available, while a quiet chat with the newsagent himself will prove very useful, since he will probably have advance information about new teenage magazines which are being launched. And of course, to give you greater depth and understanding of what is required, all you have to do is talk to any teenage members of your family – or those of your friends. They'll be eager to tell you what kind of stories they enjoy reading – and why. Frankly, I consider that forming an understanding relationship with adolescents is essential; not

1

only will they tell you how they feel about things and give you some insight into how they 'tick' – that's in case you've forgotten your own teenage years – they'll also provide you with themes and ideas to write about.

The same is true of novels. About ten years ago, several major British publishers – Heinemann and Macmillan, for instance – were publishing both hardback and paperback novels for teenagers. Then, quite suddenly, for some inexplicable reason, the bottom fell out of the market and several of my friends who were at the time writing successfully for that specialised market were left high and dry.

Several barren years resulted. And then, Bantam, the American publishers, brought out a series called 'Sweet Dreams'. Written by a team of highly professional authors, they were such a success that they were brought to this country to see if their appeal was universal.

If you want to discover whether they were or not, just take a look at the teenage section of any bookshop in your town. You'll probably discover that the series is displayed on a revolving stand. A closer look at the novels themselves will reveal that they are numbered as well as titled. There can be one reason only for this: their readers have such confidence in the novels issued under that imprint that they will buy blindly – by merely quoting the numbers of issues they have still to read. Indeed, I have actually heard a grandmother checking a list given by a granddaughter and asking for the book by its number only.

That is the pinnacle of success.

It wasn't long before British publishers realised that there was a gap in the market. Pan Books brought out their Heartline Series, followed recently by Penguin, Methuen and Corgi, producing novels written specially for teenagers and catering for their emotional as well as literary needs. By the time this book is published there may be more. And I'm talking only of the paperback market. There are some hardback firms which also publish books for teenagers. Your local librarian will tell you which and advise you which are the most popular.

And that brings us to what kind of novels teenagers like to read. They like books about people like themselves, with characters they can identify with, in locations and situations which excite them and which at the same time prepare them for the adult world they are eager to enter. Strangely, though market research seems to indicate that they are obsessed with 'raw sex', when it comes to buying, they go for the more romantic novels. I mean, of course, romance in its widest sense. And that observation comes from a bookshop owner I am friendly with, who keeps a large and varied display of teenage novels. It is the gentler novels they seem to like, he said; they seem to prefer the more emotional stories – an indication perhaps of the factors that are most important to them at a highly emotional stage in their lives.

Perhaps it would be wise at this stage to consider the characteristics of adolescence, because unless we understand the needs and problems, both emotional and physical, of young people at a crucial stage in their lives, then we cannot possibly produce work which will interest them, nor will we be able to have sympathy and empathy with them. I don't have to tell you how infuriatingly difficult adolescents can be; we've all suffered from them and begin to wonder why we bothered to have children in the first place. It might have been better to breed cats and dogs instead – so I've heard said.

But hold on. If you've ever thought like that, it might be an idea to cast your mind back to the days of your

3

own youth. Remember those heady days of summer when you walked hand in hand along country lanes with a partner whose name you can't remember now – let alone what he or she looked like? Remember the glorious days spent lazing on sunny beaches? Remember the discos? We called them dances, didn't we? I don't think the word was in vogue at that time and I certainly hadn't heard of 'gigs'. Remember the certainty that this life was yours to do with as you wished; a life you were determined to live to the full, creating your own successes, making your own mistakes? Remember the way you planned to conquer the whole world? Remember the tears and the pain and the heartache?

REMEMBER HOW INFURIATINGLY DIFFI-CULT YOUR MOTHER AND FATHER COULD BE?

Remembering that came as a shock, didn't it? Never-theless, if it did, at least we're getting somewhere. At least, you're beginning to re-inhabit the world of the adolescent.

O.K. Let's look closer at teenagers. What, then, are the characteristics of adolescence?

First there is an expansion – an explosion almost – of emotions, both in range and intensity. Adolescents will cry at the drop of a hat or at the receipt of a sharp rebuke, at which point, life isn't worth living; they are, alternately, confused, scared, moody and quarrelsome. Fortunately, for them and for us, the depression does not last long; within minutes they are laughing again and bursting with enthusiasm as, with fresh make-up applied to eyes that are remarkably free of conjunctivitis, they rush down the stairs, departing to meet the guy who phoned and vanishing quickly into the night in case mum or dad start asking awkward questions and making ridicu-lous demands about getting home early.

Things – issues, problems, relationships and their reaction to them – really matter; everything is seen in black and white; decisions to be made are clear-cut. There is no room for doubt or compromise. And it is that attitude that makes teenagers appear so arrogant at times. Of course, we adults smile rather smugly and say to ourselves: 'You've got a lot to learn. Wait till you're my age. Then you'll know.'

And of course we're right. But we were like that once too, and if we hadn't demanded the right to make our own mistakes, then we would never have learned, would we? We wouldn't be able to say: 'Wait till you're my age. Then you'll know.'

Secondly, though there is a love of life and an arrogant self-confidence which constantly manifests itself, it is only skin deep. Literally. Remember what it was like to have a spot on your face before going out on a date? Or the girl you fancied chose another guy? (The opposite is true for lady readers, of course!) The whole world collapsed in on you. It was a catastrophe unparalleled in the history of the human race. It was at that time you most needed support but didn't get it from unsympathetic parents – *your* parents – who told you that boys and girls are like London buses: if you lose one, there's another coming behind.

Did you believe them? Of course you didn't. And you vowed there and then that when you had children of your own, you'd never treat them in such an appalling way. I wonder if you kept that promise.

Thirdly, there is a longing for new exciting experiences. That is why teenagers so often experiment with drugs and drink. They are not prepared to accept the dire warnings with which we adults caution them. They want to savour the experience for themselves and then decide if they'll

5

continue with it. Many heed the warnings, of course, having MADE UP THEIR MINDS FOR THEM-SELVES, and I suppose one of the most optimistic factors facing us is the awareness that most of the young people who do experiment come out of the experience relatively unscathed.

Fourthly, the need for independence is so strong that they often challenge our authority. They instinctively feel, deep inside, that they have to assert themselves; they feel they have to fight to prove themselves. I know only too well that it can be very annoying to have advice questioned if not completely disregarded; it can be very frustrating and wearying to have constant arguments in the house. But we should remember that this is an essential stage in their development, and if we as sensible parents make allowances for them and discuss their problems without causing rifts, then the relationship will change from that of offspring to that of friend. I honestly believe that the arguments are essential for that to occur, but also am convinced that it is important to be logical rather than scathing. After all, just cast your mind back and remember how deeply unjust criticism affected your confidence; in spite of your bravado, that confidence was as fragile as an egg-shell. Things haven't changed; teenagers are still as unsure of themselves as ever they were.

Fifthly, they are searching for identity. They are no longer submissive sons and daughters; they are PEOPLE IN THEIR OWN RIGHT. They demand the right to 'do their own thing' and insist on doing it even if we disapprove. I remember walking through the town centre with my adolescent daughter one Saturday afternoon and came across two teenagers walking hand in hand, tatty in worn jeans with hair spiky and dyed a brilliant orange.

'Look at those two!' I said. I'm sure there must have been a note of disapproval in my voice.

For the first time in years, my daughter obeyed me and looked. Her eyes became large and luminous and there was a delighted grin on her lips.

'Yeah! Great, isn't it!' she replied.

That shook me. 'Williams,' I said silently to myself. 'You're getting old. You really think you're going to be able to write for these kids?'

That's when I decided to become a born-again teenager.

You should try it sometime; it's fantastic. Or is it 'fab' now?

Sixthly, there is an overwhelming desire to master all the social skills that the adult world will expect of them. But they are not going to prepare themselves for the world of their parents. They are not going to make the same mistakes. No way. Their world is going to be better, because they are going to conquer it. And allied closely to this, of course, is the need to be accepted by their peer groups. That is the reason for gangs; they gain strength from each other; they make their own rules – often more restrictive and more demanding than those we try to impose on them. BUT THEY ARE THEIR RULES.

And seventh – and perhaps most important of all – is the instinctive demand of sex and coming to terms with it. During adolescence the sex drive is at its strongest; and yet there is a strange fear of it – until they've mastered it. Perhaps that is why, during early teens, they go around in foursomes. Perhaps it's an emotional and physical protection; if things go too far, they can literally call for help. It is during later teens that true pairing-off occurs.

When you consider it, they have a lot of skills to master in a relatively short time – so many obstacles to conquer.

7

It is no wonder that they react, sometimes violently, to the inconsistencies that they see practised by adults. Think of the father who perhaps helps himself to some object from work – a spanner from the workshop, some paper and pens from the office, or the small length of timber he needs to repair his garden shed. In other words, the things he steals from his employer. What would his reaction be if he discovered that his son or daughter had been caught shoplifting? Would he reprimand them severely, I wonder? And if his son or daughter was aware of his own thefts, can you imagine what his or her reaction would be when reprimanded?

Is it any wonder that teenagers often rebel?

It is important, therefore, if you really do wish to write for teenagers, to understand them, to know what makes them 'tick', to support and commiserate with them when they make mistakes, to remember what it was like to be in a constant state of turmoil, to experience a seething mass of conflicting emotions. It is even more important to have empathy and understand the reasons for their apparently motiveless intransigence. Not to mention their lack of appreciation for all that we adults have done for them since the moment of their birth. But they didn't ask to be born, did they?

How often have we adults had that one thrown at us?

O.K. So I've convinced you. You've got to have sympathy and empathy and infinite patience and understanding. What else?

As far as the actual mechanics of writing is concerned, it is important not to write down to them. It is equally important not to write with your tongue in your cheek or pretend that you have the necessary sympathy. You have to be sincere because teenagers are perceptive; they can spot a phoney ten miles away.

So write simply, sincerely, and, if you can, humorously. Go for emotion. Get inside your characters, feel as they feel, and write with conviction so that your readers will say: 'Yeah. That's how I feel too.' Get that reader-identification which is all-important. Create believable characters – warts and all – with whom your readers can sympathise and care about. Go on. Relive your life; enjoy yourself.

And if you can do all that, you're well on your way to success. All you have to do is plan and write those stories which will bring you wealth and fame.

2

THE TEENAGE SHORT STORY

There are basically two kinds of teenage short stories: those that portray one or two characters in one incident (these are usually quite short, about one thousand words long); they may sometimes be introspective or 'mood' stories where the heroine is recalling a romantic or emotional event. The second kind are the 'plotted' stories which consist of a series of incidents leading to a crisis in which the main character learns a truth about herself and changes because of it. This element of change is an essential ingredient of this type of story.

Here are some of the stories I've read recently in current editions of the magazines I've been studying:

1. Jane fancies Mike – with whom she is friendly – but doesn't think she stands a chance with him because he's so good-looking. But when Jeff makes a play for Jane at a party, Mike drags her outside and tells her he likes her very much. She gets the guy she really fancies.

2. Sue has a flatmate, Fran, who takes up cookery as a hobby and uses her as a guinea pig. Sue is taken ill with food poisoning. When she gets out of hospital, she discovers Fran is now into crochet and has made her a scarf which is more like a rope. She wonders if Fran is trying to strangle her. (As you will have guessed, this was a humorous story written in three scenes.)

11

3. Jackie falls for Steve, the lead singer in a local band. Everything is fine while he is struggling to make it, but when he hits the big time, their relationship deteriorates. Then disaster comes when police raid a party they're attending and she is arrested. But all publicity is good publicity for Steve. He leaves her and goes to work in America. (This was a longer, more heavily plotted story.)

If you examine the above storylines, you will see that they involve problems of relationship where, except for the second one, the boyfriend is an important factor. You will also notice that they do not all have happy endings – which is an important point to consider – though even so, it is equally important that the reader has sympathy with the jilted heroine. After all, there but for the Grace of God. . . .

Many writers are able to write both kinds of stories. Others are better at one rather than the other, and if you would like to find out which you prefer to write, the only way to do so is to learn from experience: try both kinds and discover which kind suits you.

But whichever kind you decide to write, there is one thing all writers have to do – and that is market research.

Many newcomers to writing think of an idea, work out the plot, write it and then look for a market. They take a shot in the dark. It is no wonder therefore that nine times out of ten, they miss their target.

Much better to have an idea, search for a market that will take such a story and then write for that market.

Better still to decide on a particular magazine, discover the kinds of stories it publishes, find an idea and then write it up. In this way, you see your market, aim for it

– and with a little bit of luck and a big slice of talent, you hit it.

But how, you may ask, do you go about researching a particular market?

The answer is simple and logical.

First of all, search the shelves of your local newsagent's for all the teenage magazines he stocks and for which you think you would like to write. Then buy a copy of every magazine published and read the stories for enjoyment. If any magazine publishes just one short story a week – the others may be photo-stories where the storyline is in the form of photographs with the dialogue in balloons – then it will be necessary to read that magazine for several weeks before going on to the next step: to see if a pattern emerges. As a matter of fact, it might be wise to do this irrespective of how many stories are published in each edition. It might also be a good idea to check your latest copy of the *Writers' and Artists' Yearbook* just in case your newsagent does not stock all teenage magazines, find out which are being currently published and order them. Remember to keep a record of what they cost; when you are successful, the money you have spent doing your market research can be claimed against tax.

The second step is to read through every story again. Then estimate the number of words in each and establish (a) the range in terms of length of stories published (for example, the shortest story may be less than a thousand words while the longest may be 4,000 words long) and (b) the most popular length. For example, if a magazine publishes five short stories a week, there may be one short story of a thousand words, one short story of 4,000 words, but three short stories of 2,500 words. It is a fair assumption therefore that you have more chance of selling stories which are 2,000 words long. This may seem rather clinical but if it is your intention to be professional, then it is only wise to increase your chances of success by submitting stories of the most popular length.

I know what you are now going to ask: do you have to count every word in every short story? The answer is simple. No.

You can apply one of two methods.

First, choose any ten lines in the story, preferably ten lines which contain both narrative and dialogue.

Then count the number of words in those ten lines and divide that number by ten. That will give you the average number of words per line.

Finally, count the number of lines in the story and multiply that number by the number of words in each line. You will now have a good idea of the length of that story.

Alternatively, you may measure one inch of print, again ensuring that there is a fair proportion of both narrative and dialogue, and count the number of words in that inch of print. Then measure the number of column inches that the story takes up. Finally multiply the number of column inches by the number of words in an inch of column, and you have an approximate number of words in the story.

Of course, like any estimate, it is approximate, but nevertheless it will give you a good idea of the length of any story.

The third step is to analyse each story according to the market research profile given below, and keep a careful record in a notebook. Personally, I like to record on one page and keep the opposite page blank. Later, when I read over the information gathered and a pattern emerges, the storyline may trigger off an original idea of my own. I immediately record it on the blank page; if I

14

don't I might well forget it. I also keep one notebook for every magazine I study.

Market Research Profile

Title:

Length:

Names of main characters:

Name of viewpoint character:

Ages of main characters:

Social class/occupation of main characters:

Written in 1st/3rd person:

Plot (in about 50 words):

Are the stories sad or happy?

Are the endings sad or happy?

Do the stories contain a flashback?

What is the proportion of narrative to dialogue:

You will now have a very good idea of the kind of stories the magazines publish, the kinds of characters they like, their names and ages, whether they are working-class or middle-class, whether they are clerks, nurses, shop assistants, unemployed, and whether they prefer their main characters to be male or female. You will also discover the kinds of themes and plots they like and whether

15

they like stories containing more dialogue than narrative, or vice versa.

At this stage, you may already have decided which magazine – or magazines – you would most like to write for.

So let's get on to the next step. Let's make a deeper analysis of each story.

Read through each story again and divide each story into its separate scenes. I find it useful to have a red pen at my side and draw a line where one scene ends and another begins. Do this even for those transitional pieces of narrative which link one major scene with another. You will find a more detailed explanation of this procedure in the next chapter dealing with the 'real life' or 'confession' story.

Next, take another notebook and write down BRIEF-LY what happens in each scene. By doing this, you will see how the plot progresses and you should gain insight into the way each story is constructed. Then answer the following questions:

1. Where does the story begin?

2. Which characters are introduced in the first scene?

3. What is the problem facing the main character?

4. Is this problem stated or shown in the first scene? If not, where is it stated?

5. Does each scene proceed logically from the preceding scene?

6. Is there a flashback?

7. If so, in which scene does it begin and in which scene does it end?

16

8. How does the story end?

9. Does the main character have a relationship problem? If so, with whom does the main character have a relationship problem and what is its nature?

9. Does the main character change in any way by the end of the story?

10. If so, describe how he or she changes.

Having analysed several stories and answered the above questions about each one, you should gain an even deeper insight into the way those stories are constructed. Usually, you will notice that each story starts (a) at a high point where the reader's attention is captured, (b) where the main characters are introduced, and (c) where the problem the main character has to resolve is stated in its most dramatic form.

All this analysis may seem tedious, or perhaps you feel that it serves no useful purpose. However, I believe such precise study is a necessary part of any writer's learning process; it is essential to examine how successful writers – the ones whose stories you have just read – have mastered the craft of story-telling and construction, because only then can the learner successfully construct his or her own short story. It is this process of learning which is essential before any advance can be made. After all, you would not expect a doctor to learn his professional skills in any haphazard way; you would certainly expect him to put in a considerable amount of study and practice before he was let loose on an unsuspecting public.

So it is with a professional writer. If he or she is to produce work that the readership enjoys and avoid those soul-destroying rejection slips, then detailed, searching study is essential. After all, you are not writing for yourself; you are writing for your readers – and you owe them your best.

Up until now, you have been involved with analysis; you have been breaking down published stories into their component parts – just as early anatomists dissected bodies – to see how they are constructed.

I'm sure you'll have learned a great deal.

Now comes synthesis; the building up of a story from your own original idea – a much more exciting prospect. But first let's deal with something many newcomers to writing ask: where do you get your ideas?

I've already indicated one source of ideas; the reading of published short stories will trigger off an idea of your own. It may be that you are unimpressed with the story you have read and believe you could write a better one on a similar theme; or you may not be convinced either with the characterisation in a particular story or the way the plot develops. Whatever the reason, by playing around with an idea, you could well develop a completely different story to the one you have read.

The problem pages of magazines will often provide you with plots, tailor-made for those particular magazines. They will indicate the situations in which the readers find themselves, the problems they face – and the advice given will tell you what the ethos of the magazine is. What you have to do is dramatise the problem by creating characters who will act out the story. Try it. It is an extremely good exercise which will teach you a great deal.

Look out for items in your daily or weekly newspaper. They are always a good source of human interest stories and teenagers seem always to be in the news these days. But always try to get behind the stories which are reported; pretend that you are the person involved and try to imagine what factors led up to the event which was reported. Try to understand the motives of the participants and look at the story from the angle of each person involved. By doing so, you may well end up with quite a different story from the one reported.

Another valuable source of ideas comes from listening to gossip. After all, items of gossip are full of human interest; otherwise who would be interested in what Mrs Jones from round the corner did when the insurance man called? Or in the case of the teenager, what a certain boyfriend would do if he discovered that his girlfriend, the typist at the next desk, was meeting someone else when he was at the local Tech. But why was she meeting this guy? What's wrong with her relationship with the steady boyfriend?

If you travel by bus or train, listen to what – or rather, whom – the people next to you are talking about, taking care of course not to make it obvious. Items of gossip can trigger off some fantastic ideas for short stories, provided you don't feel obliged to stick to the truth. Ask yourself: what would I do in those circumstances? Or better still: WHAT IF?

What if the typist's boyfriend went to the pub and found his girlfriend there with another guy? What if he had taken another girl there? What if he was the jealous type and picked a fight with the other fella? Only to find the meeting an innocent one? The possibilities are endless, depending on the originality of your own answers.

Try twisting an original story by changing the sex of your main character; try to see the situation from his or her angle. His or her reaction and subsequent action will create quite a different story; the plot will probably develop in such a way that the new story bears little

19

resemblance to the old. It is not cheating to do this. There are, after all, a limited number of plots, themes, problems, situations and storylines. I was once given a storyline by one of the editors I worked for and discovered that it had already been used in a previous edition of the story. I referred back to her and she calmly told me to go ahead and write it because she was sure it would be a different story.

She was right – and the reason was simple. My main character was quite different from the one in the original story and therefore the finished story was different too. I had learned a valuable lesson: characters create plot.

Finally, don't neglect songs and song titles. The titles can trigger off new ideas while the actual words can often provide ready-made plots. All you have to do is provide the character, the scene and the action. The rest will be simple.

Now back to the nitty-gritty. Now is the time to build up; you've done your analysis; now comes synthesis. Do you remember in our first session how, in the market research profile, I asked you to write the basic plot of the story you were studying – in about fifty words? That is the next thing you should do.

Start with a name and a brief description of the characters and plot. For example:

This is the story of Jane Wardley, a sixteen-year-old girl who has been working at a supermarket for the last three months. She has a boyfriend, Dave, who is unemployed. Then, Mark comes to work at the supermarket as a trainee supervisor. She falls for him – and he for her. What should she do about Dave?

Can you see how I've decided already on my viewpoint

character, Jane, set the scene, and given her a problem to overcome? All she has to do is solve it. What she does to solve it – the actions she takes, and the reactions of others – creates the plot. I also decide how the story is going to end.

The next stage is to see the characters as clearly as possible. I let them whirl around in my mind; I let them react to each other; I let them 'speak' to me. Once I hear them speak and, in my mind, see them act and react, I take a sheet of paper and list the scenes as they occur to me. I state BRIEFLY what happens in each scene. Then I ask myself the following questions:

1. Is the sequence of events correct?

2. Is each action logical?

3. Is each action feasible?

4. Are the actions in character? This is an extremely important question; the success of the whole story depends on the answer being 'yes'.

5. Have I constructed an interesting story?

6. Can it be improved? If so, how?

I HAVE NOW CREATED MY STORY PLAN AND AM READY TO WRITE MY STORY. SO NATURALLY, I START AT THE BEGINNING.

I work systematically, writing every scene until eventually I reach the end of the story.

It is at this point that I ask myself a most important question: have I started at the right place? Have I started:

21

(a) at a high point in the story where the reader's attention is hooked?

(b) where the main characters are introduced? and

(c) where the viewpoint character's problem is stated in its most dramatic form?

If the answer is yes, then I have no worries. If the answer is no, then I have to decide where the right place to start is, bearing in mind the three points I have stated above.

I usually find that I have already written the scene which satisfies all these requirements; it may be in the middle of the first draft or it may be near the end. It does not really matter where it is; all I have to do is transfer it to the beginning – an easy enough procedure with a word processor. Rather more difficult without, I agree, but one that will bring dividends.

The next step is to revise. I look at my opening paragraph and see if it contains the five W's. I ask the following questions:

WHO are the main characters?

WHERE are they?

WHAT are they doing?

WHERE are they doing it?

WHY are they doing it?

If I have answers for all those questions, I know I have given the reader all the information he or she requires. I then read the whole story and decide if it has the right 'feel' to it. It's difficult to explain exactly what I mean by that; it may be partly intuition, partly experience – and

I don't necessarily mean writing experience. I use my experience as a reader at this point. I ask myself if the story is sufficiently interesting. I have to stand back and examine it as if I'm reading it for the first time – and if I 'feel' that something is wrong, if I get a gut reaction telling me that all is not well, then I have a close look at that story and try to find out what's troubling me. Sometimes I have to leave it until the following day, and usually a night's rest – during which my mind works at a subconscious level – brings the answer I've been searching for.

I check my spelling, examine the way I express myself by reading the story aloud, and if there are any awkward passages, I revise them – usually by simplifying them.

When I am satisfied I've done my best, I submit my story, complete of course with the mandatory stamped addressed envelope. And of course, I start immediately on my next story.

It might be wise here to say a few words about photostories, an extremely profitable source of income if you can master the technique involved. The same strategy should be adopted as for any other kind of writing: do your market research as stated earlier, only this time count the number of frames they use for their stories – but be careful; the number of frames used may well change so it is important to keep your reading up to date.

It is wise to study each story according to the profile I've already given you and then do a more detailed analysis. Number each frame and write down briefly (a) where the action takes place, (b) which characters are present, (c) what is happening, and, most importantly, (d) what they are saying.

I've stressed the importance of dialogue because although the reader can actually see the characters, she can discover what that character is really like only through dialogue. It has to be economical and true. Notice that captions are used sparingly and only where necessary, that expensive locations are usually avoided and that each story has a small cast. Moreover, since the actors have to be paid, all those actors have to be present for a large proportion of the story. It is not wise, economically, to introduce a character into just one or two frames and then for that character to be discarded. Each character must be essential to the plot.

When you've analysed a story, you have the format for writing the scripts, so the next step is to try writing them yourself.

If you really are interested and would like more information, a letter to the Photo Story Editor (MW), D. C. Thomson and Co. Ltd, Courier Buildings, Dundee, DD1 9QJ will bring you their excellent tip-sheet entitled *Some Hints on Writing Photo-Stories*.

It will tell you all you need to know about photo-story writing.

And finally a few words about the technique of using flashbacks. This is a technique that newcomers to the short story find difficult, yet it is really a simple matter to master. It is basically achieved by altering the tense of your verbs so that you start out telling what has happened in the past and then go on quickly as though it is actually happening at the present.

Look at this example:

I put on the kettle and walking wearily into the living room, slumped into the armchair. I closed my eyes tightly, trying desperately to stem the tears that were already welling up.

It was only six months since Barry and I HAD MET. I

HAD GONE to the local disco and as soon as I HAD WALKED in, he HAD COME over and HAD ASKED me to dance. . . .

I have exaggerated the tenses of the sentences to emphasise what I am trying to show. All this is happening in the past. Now watch what happens.

'I haven't seen you here before,' he SAID.

Notice that I have not used the word 'had' at this point. The action is now taking place in the 'now' of the story.

'I was here last week,' I REPLIED. I remembered seeing him and thinking how great he looked.

I hope I've made my point clearly. As I said earlier, the flashback technique involves a subtle change of tense.

Study the way successful authors use the technique because once mastered, it will prove a simple and invaluable literary device to use.

3

WRITING THE TEENAGE CONFESSION STORY

Though the teenage confession story – sometimes called the 'real life' story – is basically the same as any other short story, nevertheless it differs from the more conventional story in several respects.

Look at some of the advice given below from a tip-sheet issued by one of the teenage confession magazines:

'I have done wrong; I've learned from my mistakes; and now, by describing it to you, I'm helping you to learn from it too.'

'That is the spirit and purpose of the real-life story – and that too should be its style. Therefore the stories are written in the first person, and they must have the immediacy and conviction of personal accounts of genuine experiences. And the narrators must be people with whom the readers can easily identify – they must be just like themselves.'

'Fundamentally, the real life story should convey a helpful message about life and human relationship.'

'The stories should leave the reader emotionally satisfied, whether or not the ending is happy. Justice must prevail in the end and the confessing heroine must have learned from the experience. However, there is no need

to sermonise; the moral should reveal itself without pro-
longed reflection and analysis.'

The above quotations are from the guidelines issued by
the editor of a 'real life magazine', and though there is
now a change in style and requirement, nevertheless, the
advice given is still correct. The stories

1. are about ordinary people with ordinary problems
    in ordinary situations.

2. are written in the first person.

3. are written in an intimate, 'gossipy' style so as to
    give the impression to the reader that the heroine is
    actually telling her story.

4. demand that the main character comes to an
    understanding of her problem and of the flaw in
    her character or attitude of mind that created it and
    CHANGES at the end.

5. do not necessarily have a happy ending BUT
    SHOULD ALWAYS PROVIDE HOPE FOR
    THE FUTURE.

Before writing a 'real life story', it is essential yet again
to carry out your market research to discover what kind
of story a particular magazine demands. You will find
that some magazines require a more abrasive kind, both
in the kind of themes they prefer and in the way they are
written. Others insist on gentler, less dramatic stories
where the emphasis is on depth of characterisation. The
writer should therefore read several copies of the maga-

zine of his or her choice and complete the market research profile suggested earlier, but with some additions.

Title of story:

Length:

Names of main characters:

Name of viewpoint character:

Ages of characters:

Social class/occupations:

Location of story:

Problem main character has to solve/overcome:

Character flaw or attitude of main character:

Brief description of plot:

If a flashback is used, note its length, where it begins and where it ends.

Analysing the stories in this way will not only provide you with an accurate knowledge of the length and type of story required but give you a good idea of the style of writing required. It is wise to study and practise this style. Incidentally, never write with your tongue in your cheek; you will not convince. You must not only believe in your character and sympathise with her and her problem; you must be that character. In that way, you will write sincerely, convincingly and so provide the reader-identification which is essential.

You will find that there are two kinds of construction as far as confession stories are concerned:

1. There is the chronological story where you start at the beginning and work through to the end.

2. Then there is the story that contains a flashback. In this type of story, you start, as I've stated earlier, at a high point somewhere in the middle, flashback to the beginning, and then work through to the end. This is a very popular method because by starting at a high point in the story, you grab the reader's attention – and this is so important since it affects sales. Of course, there is no reason why a chronological story should not start at a high point too.

Which brings us to our next consideration: where to start?

As stated earlier, beginnings should always be dramatic. At the risk of repeating myself, they should start at a HIGH POINT in the story in order to capture the interest of the reader, where the main characters are introduced and where the problem is revealed in its most dramatic form. Go for CONFLICT and EMOTION.

There is no better way to learn this technique than by examining how the experts do it. So:

1. Choose a story – a long one preferably – and read it.

2. Then, with a red pen, go through it a second time and draw a line after every scene.

3. Write on a sheet of paper BRIEFLY what happens in every scene.

4. Note when a flashback occurs and how it is done.

5. Note how the story returns to the present.

6. Note how the story ends.

7. Ask yourself: what problem did the heroine face?

8. Ask yourself: what character flaw or bad attitude did the heroine possess?

9. Ask yourself: how and why did she change at the end of the story?

BY DOING THIS, YOU WILL LEARN THE ART OF SHORT STORY CONSTRUCTION.

Let us look at the example given below. You will notice that I have divided the story into several scenes and that it contains a flashback.

(1) It was raining heavily as I waited in the bus shelter at the end of Phil's street. I knew I shouldn't be doing what I was doing – that I should trust Phil – but I loved him so much that I just had to know the truth.

As I peered round the corner of the shelter for the twentieth time, he came out of the house. Tall with fair wavy hair, he slammed the door behind him and strode down the path. Just seeing him made a hard lump come to my throat. I stepped back quickly, my heart thumping like mad inside me, hoping that he hadn't seen me. Then, carefully, I glanced out again. He was getting into his car now and only then did I notice the bunch of flowers in his hand.

So I was right. He was two-timing me. He was seeing someone else on a Sunday afternoon. Anger flashed inside me as my stomach twisted with jealousy. I wanted to run over there and then and tell him exactly what I thought of him.

But he was already driving away and there was no way I could follow him.

*

(2)   I wandered dejectedly back home, bitter tears welling into my eyes, ignoring the rain that soaked me to the skin. I loved Phil; I loved him more than life itself. And he had said he loved me. Often.

So why was he treating me like this? I kept asking myself over and over again.

I slipped out of my wet clothes and huddled in front of the gas fire wondering what he was doing at that moment. Kissing her, probably. When he should have been kissing and loving me.

*

(3 – THE FLASHBACK)   I filled a kettle, switched it on and threw myself on to the settee. Phil and I HAD BEEN going steady for several months ever since that first night we met at the disco. I'D BEEN between boyfriends at the time and after my experience with Gavin, I was in no mood to go steady again.

But then someone TAPPED me on my shoulder and looking round, I found myself gazing into the most fantastic blue eyes I'd ever seen.

'Fancy a dance,' he asked, giving me a grin that made every nerve in my body tingle.

And that was it. I was smitten again. He took me home and we started going steady and for the first few months, everything was great. But gradually I'd become suspicious. The trouble was, whenever I asked him to come round to tea on a Sunday afternoon, he always refused.

'I like to do some work on a Sunday, Helen,' he'd say, unable to look me fully in the eyes. He was a building science student at the local Tech and went there two evenings a week. 'I'll never get my diploma if I don't.'

Gradually, I became more and more certain that wasn't the real reason. He never met me on the Tech nights either and it often made me wonder what he did after lectures. His excuse that he went out with his mates for a pint didn't convince me. So I started wondering where he went to and every time I came up with the same answer.

32

He was seeing someone else.

In the end, I couldn't stand it any longer. I had to find out once and for all what was going on. So I found myself waiting outside his flat, spying on him.

*

(4 – RETURN TO PRESENT.) The sound of a whistling kettle brought me out of my reverie and I rushed to switch it off. As I sipped my coffee, I breathed in deeply and sighed. Now I knew for certain. Phil was two-timing me. So what was I going to do about it?

*

(5) The following evening when I went round to his flat, I decided to find out who she was. Once, when he'd been paying for some drinks down the pub, I'd seen this photograph in his wallet. So when he went to make some coffee, I picked up his jacket and took it out.

For a moment, I hesitated. I knew that what I was doing was wrong; that I was being deceitful and horrible but I couldn't help it. I loved him and I couldn't bear to think of him being with another girl. Taking a deep breath, I took a quick look inside. There tucked away was a photograph of a girl about the same age as me with long fair hair, a beautiful oval face and light blue eyes that seemed to laugh even though her face was serious. On it she had written,

'To Phil, with all my love, Anne.'

I felt an icy hand clutch my heart as I stared at it. She was beautiful; she really was. Much prettier than me. Whatever doubts I had, had vanished. Now I had the proof. Tears began to sting my eyes when the door opened and Phil returned.

'Here's your coffee,' he announced. Then he hesitated as he sensed that I was upset. 'Hey! What's wrong?'

I turned accusingly. 'You know very well what's wrong.'

'No I don't . . .' He hesitated again as his eyes went to my hand and saw the wallet I was clutching. 'What have you got there?' he asked quietly. His expression was grave.

I was angry now, really angry. 'This,' I said, flinging the photograph at him. It fluttered in the air and landed face up on the carpet.

He picked it up, took the wallet from my trembling hands and replaced it.

'Aren't you going to say anything?' I demanded.

He shrugged his shoulders. 'What's to say?'

For a moment, I was speechless. I just stared at him as fury surged up inside me. 'What's to say? I find a photograph of another girl in your wallet, and that's all you can say.'

'It's just somebody I . . . I knew once.'

'Knew? Don't kid me. You're still seeing her.'

My words shocked him. 'What makes you say that?' he said.

His reply made me even more furious. 'Don't be stupid, Phil. I saw you. Yesterday. Taking her flowers. Don't try and deny it.' I paused for a moment waiting for him to say something. 'Aren't you going to tell me who she is?'

He turned away from me. 'Her name's Anne,' he said.

'Oh great!' I replied scornfully. 'Tell me something I don't know.'

'There's nothing to tell.' He turned and looked me straight in the eye. 'She doesn't mean anything to me . . . not any more. It's you I love.'

'Yet you see her. Every Sunday.'

He shook his head. 'It's not what you think,' he said.

'Not what I think? What am I to think? You don't deny the flowers were for her, do you?'

'No. I don't.'

'Or that you have been seeing her. I want the truth, Phil.'

'I'm telling you the truth.' He paused. 'I have been seeing her. In a way. But honestly, there's nothing to worry about. Please trust me, Helen. Please.'

I wanted to trust him. I really did. But I felt so betrayed that all I wanted to do was hurt him back.

'How can I, Phil?' I said bitterly. I picked up my coat and flung it over my shoulders. 'How can I ever trust you again?'

*

34

(6) I stormed out of the flat, pushing him away when he tried to stop me.

Afterwards, as I lay on my bed so miserable that I wanted to die, I wished that I had let him stop me, that he'd made me believe him when he said there was nothing to worry about. But he was asking too much. If I didn't love him, it wouldn't have mattered. But I did love him, more than he would ever know, and that was all there was to it.

*

(7) The next day though, when he phoned me at work, I jumped at the chance of meeting him again. But when he called round, I was so churned up I couldn't behave naturally to him. I couldn't enjoy his kisses and it showed. Then, after he'd held me in his arms and got no response, he pushed himself to his feet.

'You're still thinking about Anne, aren't you?' he said.

'Of course I am!' I muttered, evading his eyes.

He took a deep breath. 'Very well, then. I don't suppose you'll be satisfied until you know the whole truth.' He picked up his jacket and shrugged his arms into the sleeves. 'Come on, let's go.'

I looked up in alarm. 'Where . . . where are you taking me?'

'I'm taking you to see Anne.'

Suddenly I got scared. Meeting her was the last thing in the world I wanted. 'No. I'm not going.'

He grabbed my arm. 'Oh, yes you are. You wanted to know who she is. Now you're going to find out.'

He virtually forced me down the stairs to his car and held me tightly with one hand until he'd pulled away from the kerb. I was scared. Really scared. I didn't want to meet Anne. I didn't want to come face to face with her. Suddenly, I wished I'd believed him, trusted him. But it was too late now for regrets.

I sat hunched in the seat as he drove along, my stomach churning with apprehension, a hard lump in my throat.

*

(8)   He didn't drive far. Just a mile or two out of town on the London road – until he came to a small churchyard. He pulled up outside, got out of the car and opened the door for me.

'Why . . . why are you stopping here?' I stammered.

'To see Anne,' he said simply.

My mind spun. Surely he hadn't arranged to meet Anne when he was seeing me. And why here? I asked myself. Had he arranged to meet her in the church porch? I wondered. My mind was spinning so much I couldn't think properly.

He led me firmly up the path towards the church as I clung to him, my legs turning to jelly under me. I couldn't see anyone in the porch. Unless she was sitting on one of the benches, out of sight.

But before he got there, he stopped.

'Here she is,' he said simply.

I looked around an empty churchyard. 'Where?'

'Here!' He nodded to a small grave. 'This is where I meet her. Every Sunday afternoon.'

I looked at the engraving on the small wooden cross. 'In loving memory of Anne Barlow,' it said. 'Died 21st November, 1985. Rest in peace.'

'It's her grave!' My voice was tight and hoarse.

He nodded. 'She died in a motorcycling accident . . .' He paused and I knew what he was going to say. 'It was my motorcycle. She was on the pillion seat.'

There was silence for a few moments; above us a slight breeze moaned softly through the yew-trees that circled the churchyard.

'Oh, Phil!' I muttered hoarsely. 'I didn't realise. Please . . . Please forgive me . . .'

'There's nothing to forgive . . .'

'Yes there is. I should have trusted you.'

He shook his head sadly. 'And I should have told you. But how could I? How could I possibly tell you that. . . .'

His words trailed off, but I knew what he was thinking. How could he possibly tell me that he had killed her. Someone he'd once loved.

I put my arm through his and leaned my head against his shoulder.

'Oh Phil!' I whispered. 'I do love you. So much.'

He smiled down at me, then kissed me gently on my forehead. 'And I love you too. More than you'll ever know.' Then he breathed out a long sigh. 'I should have told you long ago. Now . . . I'm glad I have.'

*

(9)   So was I. We drove home in silence, a silence in which trust was born, and as we walked into his flat I knew that never again would I doubt him. And never again would he keep any secrets from me.

If we use the market research profile suggested, we find that the length of the story is 2,000 words, the main characters are Helen and Phil, with Helen being the view-point character. Helen is a typist while Phil is a student and the location is a small town. We discover that Helen's problem is that she believes Phil is two-timing her, while her character flaws are jealousy and lack of trust. A short flashback is used while a brief summary of the plot is simply that Helen, suspecting that Phil is two-timing her, sets out to find the truth. Finding a girl's photograph in his pocket, she accuses him of deceiving her and will not listen to his pleas. Phil takes her to see Anne – to a cemetery where she is buried and Helen discovers that Anne was a passenger on Phil's motorcycle when they were involved in an accident and she was killed. Full of remorse, she begs for forgiveness, vowing never to doubt him again.

If you examine the short story again, you will see that I have divided it into nine scenes, each one leading logically and systematically to the next. So let us examine each scene in detail and discover how the story was constructed.

Scene 1: Helen, suspecting Phil of infidelity, waits in hiding outside his house and sees him emerge carrying a bunch of flowers and drive away. Her suspicions are confirmed.

Scene 2: Helen returns home, feeling terrible.

Scene 3: Puts on kettle. A short Flashback to the time she first met him. Relationship good at first; suspicion sets in when he constantly refuses to come to tea on a Sunday.

Scene 4: Return to present when kettle whistles.

Scene 5: The following evening she goes to Phil's flat and, searching his wallet, finds Anne's photograph. Phil begs her to trust him when he says there is nothing to worry about. But she refuses and leaves.

Scene 6: She storms back to her place.

Scene 7: Next day there is a reconciliation but it is obvious that she can't get Anne off her mind. Phil insists on taking her to see Anne. Helen is scared.

Scene 8: They arrive at a churchyard. Helen is confused, thinks they are to meet her in the church porch. But Phil points at a gravestone. Anne's. He tells her how she died – when she was on the pillion seat of his motorcycle – and how he feels responsible for her death. Helen is ashamed of her behaviour.

Scene 9: They drive home in silence and Helen vows never to doubt Phil again.

This story was in fact planned in chronological order, that is, starting at the first night she met Phil. But it soon became obvious that it was much better to start at the point where she waited outside Phil's flat because not only did I introduce Phil and Helen but I also stated the problems she was suffering from, namely, her suspicions that Phil was two-timing her and her jealousy. It was the obvious emotional high spot.

From there the story goes on to explain her suspicion and the reason for it – that is, Phil's constant refusal to come to tea on Sundays, followed by a short flashback. Note the capital letters I have used in Scene 3; I know I've explained the method once but repetition does no harm.

Then there is confirmation of her suspicions when she does something quite unforgivable: searching Phil's wallet and finding Anne's photograph.

After their quarrel, because of their love for each other, there is a tenuous reconciliation – which does not work. Phil then reveals who Anne was and why he always refused to come to tea on Sundays.

Finally, Helen realises that she should have trusted Phil and vows never to doubt him again, thereby overcoming her character flaws: jealousy and lack of trust.

It is therefore quite a moral story, pointing out in dramatic form what can happen in a given circumstance. But nowhere is the moral stated. It is made obvious through the actions, reactions and decisions of the characters, and therefore conforms to the strict requirements of this genre.

However, though the story line and its breakdown into scenes may appear simple, it is only fair to say that a great deal of thought has gone into it. But before I deal with that, let us look at the mechanics of that flashback.

It is quite simple really.

I start with the ploy of filling the kettle because the sound of the whistle when it boils is going to bring Helen back to the present. Then I say:

Phil and I HAD BEEN going steady for several months ever since that first night we HAD MET at the disco. I'D BEEN between boyfriends at the time . . .

All this is happening in the past. In the next sentence I change the tense of the verb so that it seems that it is taking place 'now'.

But then someone TAPPED me on my shoulder . . .

Can you see the difference? At this point, Helen talks as if it is all happening in the present. It is an extremely useful technique to learn, and once you understand it, quite easy to apply.

But back to the planning stage.

There are six main stages in the writing of any story.

The first is the brief statement of the plot, the characters, the location and the problem.

The second is an in-depth investigation of the characters, their motives, and their actions and reactions. It is a time when I look at all the options open to me, i.e. I look at all the ways the characters might behave and decide on the most feasible and the most dramatic. I am, after all, trying to tell a good story. When I've made the multiple decisions I must make I go on to the next stage.

This, the third stage, is when I plan the actual story; the time when I break it down into scenes, allowing my characters to dictate – within certain parameters – the plot.

The fourth stage is when I decide where to start; at a high point where the main characters are introduced and their problem stated in its most dramatic form. If necessary, I revise my original plan.

The fifth stage is the actual writing of the story.

The sixth stage is the revision.

I have of course left out the seventh, which is the submission of the completed story.

Try this method and see if it works for you. If it doesn't, don't despair. You may, in the process, find a method of your own you can work to.

WRITING THE TEENAGE NOVEL

As I've said earlier, the teenage market is now an expanding one, especially that of the teenage novel, and therefore writing for this particular market is an exciting prospect, in some respect far more so than writing the short story. To begin with, you are able to write in depth as well as breadth; you can create more characters than you can in the short story and the plotting is more involved. And since I enjoy plotting, the experience is much more enjoyable. In addition, the range of themes investigated is wider, as are the types of stories published; for instance, there are not only teenage romances as exemplified by those novels published under the 'Sweet Dreams' imprint, but novels of adventure and mystery as well. An examination of the teenage section of your local bookseller will give you a good idea of the type and range of stories published.

The requirements expected of the novelist are basically the same as for the short story; empathy with and sympathy for the problems that adolescents encounter are vital and it is important when you write that you do so honestly, trying to understand the often perplexing situations that teenagers face and, like the short stories, you have to do this without preaching or moralising.

43

Pointing to a possible solution is as far as you should go, and of course, hope should always spring eternal.

But what, people often ask, is the difference between a short story and a novel?

It is very difficult to define and is not merely a difference in length, so it might be a useful exercise to examine two basic plots involving the same characters in virtually the same situations and experiencing the same problems, and discover if we can arrive at some valid conclusions.

The first is the plot of a short story: Jennifer, a sixteen-year-old schoolgirl, is always moaning about her mother and the way she insists on her helping with the daily and weekend chores. Her mother is taken into hospital for two days for observation and in that time, Jennifer, who has to look after her father and younger brother, realises just how much her mother did for her. She vows that when her mother is discharged from hospital, she will never again object to helping her.

If we examine this plot we discover:

1. The time span is a short one; just a few days.

2. There are few changes of scene. In fact, the only locations involved are the home and hospital.

3. There are few characters involved – just Jennifer, her mother, father and brother.

4. The story is told from one viewpoint – Jennifer's.

5. The main character is faced with one problem to overcome, her own lack of consideration for her mother.

Let us now create the plot of a novel using the same basic situation and see what differences emerge.

44

Jennifer is always moaning about her mother and the way she insists on her helping with the daily and weekend chores. She arrives home one day and discovers that her mother has been rushed into hospital and there is a suspicion that she might have tried to take her own life. Though she had been suffering occasionally from depression, her mother had given no indication to Jennifer just how ill she was and the knowledge that her mother tried to protect her makes her feel guilty.

But her problems do not end there. She has to take over the running of the home for some considerable time as well as looking after her younger brother, Ian. Even the help given to her by her best friend, Emma, and her boyfriend, Steve, is not sufficient to alleviate the pressure. Indeed, this pressure increases at school - she is about to sit her G.C.S.E. examinations that year – and she gets into trouble with one of the teachers because she cannot complete her homework in time.

In desperation, she plays truant – and meets Jago, an anti-social but amusing boy of eighteen who is the head of a motorcycling gang. She finds his tenuous friendship a release from the pressures of life – he demands nothing of her – but it is a liaison which is going to create even more problems for her.

I shall stop there but if we look at this plot we can discover several points which distinguish it from the plot of the short story:

1.   The time span is relatively long – as a matter of fact, I envisage the action taking place in a period of five or six weeks.

2.   There are several changes of scene: the home, school, hospital, Steve's house, Emma's house, Jago's

house, the neighbourhood – I will know more clearly how many when I start planning the novel.

3.   There are several characters: mother, father, Steve, Emma, the schoolteacher, the nurse, Jago and his friends, to name just the main ones.

4.   The story is told from one viewpoint: that of Jennifer. As a matter of fact, this is the only way the plot resembles that of the short story.

5.   There are many problems which Jennifer has to solve: her feelings of guilt, the way in which her school work is beginning to deteriorate, the knowledge that her father is having an affair (I've only just decided on that), her relationship with Jago and his anti-social gang. I don't think I need go on.

So while the short story is inward-looking and restrictive, the novel is outward-looking: you have to consider far more characters in several locations, who act and react to each other in a variety of ways. It is an exciting situation for the writer to find himself – or herself – in. It certainly presents more of a challenge – and that's what life is all about.

So what are the implications?

1.   Despite the broader canvas, the impact of the teenage novel must be as immediate as that of the short story. You must start at a high point in your story, where your main characters are introduced in a particular location, and where the problem your main character has to face is revealed in its most dramatic form. THE BEGINNING MUST GRIP THE READER.

2. It must go on logically from that beginning in a proper sequence of events which leads to –

3. A climax which is satisfying to the reader where –

4. The ending is not obvious, but on reflection must be inevitable.

5. The suspense must be maintained from beginning to end.

6. The action should, wherever possible, be shown not told – though there must be time for reflection, the quiet moments which I will discuss later.

7. The story must be thoroughly planned and must move quickly; economy of construction is all-important.

8. You must write and rewrite and rewrite until you are satisfied there are no loose ends or anomalies.

Just as there are differences between the short story and the novel, so there are differences between the adult and teenage novel. The most obvious difference is length; the teenage novel is generally much shorter. Though the adult novel may be anything from 55,000 words, as in the case of Mills and Boon novels, to the 250,000 words of the blockbuster, the teenage novel rarely hits the 50,000 word mark. Indeed, the length seems to be between 30,000 and 40,000 words. This must inevitably inhibit the writer to some extent, both in the complexity of his plotting and in the detail of his descriptions – and this can cause the writer some problems, not least the editing he or she has to carry out when the novel exceeds the wordage which the publisher demands. Moreover, the chapters – as well as the sentences and paragraphs – have to be shorter, with dynamic endings which will make the reader want to go on reading. And this has to be done without talking down to her.

Obviously, the main characters must be teenagers, the main one being – obviously – a girl, though it is not unusual to find novels where a boy is the viewpoint character, and since they are usually about fifteen or sixteen years old, they will usually go around in four-somes. Try to remember how you were at sixteen – and who your closest friends were. I am probably right when I predict that you went around with your best friend, her boyfriend and your boyfriend, there being safety in numbers.

As far as the readership is concerned, market research carried out by many publishing houses has shown that twelve- or thirteen-year-olds read these novels. Neverthe-less, since teenagers seem to prefer stories about people slightly older than themselves, the heroine is usually about fifteen or sixteen years old, at school or just starting work, while the hero may be eighteen. Therefore because the readership is so young, the author has a special responsibility when it comes to dealing with sexual situ-ations. One of my editors informed me quite firmly when I first started to write for her: 'No sex. The readership is too young.'

I was pleased. I had written many short stories contain-ing 'purple passages' in my endeavour to be honest, but I must admit I never liked doing so. As a teacher, I had noticed quite young girls – girls who were at an impressionable age – reading the magazines I wrote for. It worried me that they might have been reading stories with rather explicit sexual scenes in them; I had to weigh up realism against responsibility, and I have to confess that responsibility won every time. So when I was given the instruction 'No sex, please', I was more than happy to write in the way my editor wanted. I don't think the stories suffered as a result; I like to think they improved.

It is difficult to give precise advice about the length of teenage novels because not only do different publishers vary in their requirements, but those requirements can change. My present publishers gave me a maximum of 37,000 words for my first five novels; for my sixth, that maximum was lowered first to 34,000 words and finally to 31,000 words. The only thing an aspiring writer can do is write to the publishers and ask for their guidelines; they are usually more than pleased to provide you with them.

Teenagers are active people and consequently they like active stories; they like stories that have plenty of movement in them, and yet they like to have depth in characterisation as well. They like to identify – as indeed we all do – with the main character, which means that the aspiring author has to maintain a delicate balance between action and insight; that is, he or she has to get deep inside the character so that the reader will say, 'That's how I feel too!' and at the same time make the story move quickly. That is where the author has to use intuition so that the story does not become so static that it becomes boring.

Just as in the writing of short stories, it is important for the novelist to carry out market research. This can take the form, as I've just suggested, of writing to the publishers, stating your interest in writing for them and requesting their guidelines. I have never found one publisher yet who has refused, though I think I should warn you that they are busy people and sometimes replies are slow in coming.

Having done that, it is essential to read some of the novels which have already been published. A visit to your local library and a quiet word with the librarian explaining what you are looking for is often helpful. He or she will have invaluable information not only on the range of teenage novels being published, but also on the kind that teenagers like to read.

Assignment 1.

Having discovered the range of novels available, read the 'blurbs' and make a note of the kinds of plots and situations they deal with.

Here are some I have discovered myself:

1.   The girl whose parents are divorced and who reject her friends' beliefs that it is important to have a boyfriend. She reluctantly agrees to go abroad on holiday with her father – and meets a boy who captivates her.

2.   The girl whose boyfriend goes away on a school-sponsored holiday, leaving her at home. On that holiday is his ex-girlfriend. Will they get together again? she wonders. She accepts a date with another guy who likes her. But what will happen when her boyfriend finds out?

3.   The girl who lands a holiday job with an agency that manages pop groups. Normally a sensible girl, her life is transformed when she mets a lead singer who shows her another, ~~more~~ glamorous and exciting life – and she falls for him.

In all the above examples, we have the usual problems associated with adolescence: coming to terms with new situations, beliefs, and relationships. You will probably find the same when you examine the storylines you have found from your own research and you may at this stage despair at finding an idea or situation or problem which hasn't been written about. Don't despair. Stories are about people and your own characters will create a different story from situations which are basically the same as the ones you have been reading about. Frankly, I have found this exercise provides me with excellent sources of ideas, because reading the blurb of one novel will often trigger off an original idea of my own.

Assignment 2.

Read as many teenage novels as you can, preferably those published by the publisher you have already approached and analyse them using the following questionnaire:

1.   Is it written in the present time?

2.   What is the age and sex of the viewpoint character? How many main characters are there and what are their ages and sex?

3.   Is the ending happy or sad?

4.   What is the approximate length? I have found it advantageous to count the number of words on a page which contains both dialogue and narrative and then multiply that number by the number of pages in the book – even to the extent of eliminating half-pages by adding two together to make one.

5.   How many chapters are there? Are they short or long?

6. What is the proportion of narrative to dialogue?

7. How detailed are the descriptions of characters and locations?

8. What kinds of locations are described? Are they exotic?

9. Are the stories realistic or escapist? Are they fast moving? Are there any quiet moments?

10. What problems does the viewpoint character meet with? How does she cope with them?

In this way you will discover what kind of novel the publisher of your choice prefers. Make a note of the locations. You will find that the local cafe or a friend's front room are popular meeting places. So are discos, gigs and pop concerts. Start taking notice of your local teenagers and scour the local newspaper for news; you will find invaluable information about locations used by teenagers in the What's On section.

There is one important thing to remember: there'll always be teenagers. As one group become adults, another takes its place, and though fashions may change, their problems will always be the same; therefore, not only will the demand of novels be an expanding one, it will be a perennial one also.

So let us examine the technique of writing the teenage novel by considering not only themes, settings and viewpoint, but also the methods of creating believable characters; of allowing those characters to create the plots; of ways in which to convince your editor that you are capable of producing the goods, and of course the actual writing of the teenage novel.

So on to the initial idea.

Consider this one: This is the story of a sixteen-year-old girl – a keen roller-skater – who is training hard and whose ambition it is to become an international star.

So far, so good. You have an interesting situation which has, because of the heroine's desire to become an *international* star, the potential for an exciting and varied background.

But there are two important factors which are missing, namely, conflict and problem.

So let's give the girl a problem. Let us assume that she has a partner – an eighteen-year-old boy – who is equally ambitious. Let us assume that the boy has an accident during training and that he does not know when he will be fit enough to skate again, or when he is fit enough, he may not possess the necessary confidence or degree of skill to enter a competition at a late date.

That presents the girl with a problem. How is she going to compete in the pairs competition without a partner?

So now let's give her an initial solution to her problem, but one that will create further conflict.

Let us bring on to the scene, another character, another eighteen-year-old boy who is also an excellent skater. Let him be disillusioned with his present partner and be looking for a new one who is more talented. Let him be an unscrupulous young man.

What, I wonder, is he going to do when he discovers that the first girl, who is very talented, is without a partner?

I think he is going to abandon his present partner in favour of the potential new one.

But that is going to create problems. What should the first girl do when she meets with his proposal? Should she abandon her own partner? Or stand by him and wait until he recovers?

What a situation! If she waits, he may not be well in time for an important competition which is approaching. Notice I make it a few weeks rather than months in order to make it imperative that she makes a quick decision. BUT it is going to be a decision fraught with conflict.

What if her ambition – her desire to succeed – is so strong that she decides to abandon her first partner in favour of the second?

What conflict will this decision create?

(a)   The feeling of guilt at abandoning her partner.

(b)   The anger of the girl who has also been abandoned and who feels cheated.

(c)   The disapproval of her friends.

(d)   Her sorrow at losing some of her friends and the animosity shown towards her.

You can now see that we have an interesting situation which has developed through turning a problem into a potentially explosive plot with several sources of conflict.

Assignment 3.

Start with your own initial idea. Give your main characters names. Give your viewpoint character a problem which she has to solve. Let her solve it in a way which will create a moral dilemma and involve her in some kind of conflict. You will now have the embryo of an interesting story.

So on to the next stage.

5

GIVE THEM WHAT THEY WANT

When we were discussing the characteristics of adolescence in Chapter One, we were also discussing the kinds of novels that teenagers are likely to want to read. In other words, we were discussing the themes which are important to them. Therefore, it is safe to say that the themes of teenage novels have a direct relationship to the problems that adolescents face during puberty. Just as adults are interested in themes like ambition, obsessive jealousy and the effects of infidelity, so teenagers like to read stories which have a direct bearing on the problems they are facing; after all, in any good novel – even adult ones – it is possible that we all learn something from the experience of the characters involved in the stories, even if that learning is at a subconscious level. So it is with teenagers. The themes of teenage novels should relate closely to the problems encountered by adolescents during a most difficult period of their lives.

But what do we mean by *theme*?

This is a surprisingly difficult question to answer and one which many authors agonise over; I know I have. If we look in a dictionary we get the definition: 'a subject . . . written about.'

Not much help, I'm afraid. And yet, if we examine those four words closely – and one word in particular

– we might get something out of it. That one word is 'subject'.

So it could be said that the theme of a novel is the subject of the novel. But that begs another question: what do we mean by the *subject of a novel*?

Let's go back to the dictionary again. *Chambers New English Dictionary* defines 'subject' as: 'that which it is the object of the artist to express.'

Great! Now we have an object as well as a subject.

Let's look closer at the word 'object' in that definition. Surely it means 'objective'. If so, then the theme of the novel must be the objective of the novel; or to be more precise – the objective of the novelist in writing that particular novel.

So it could be argued that the theme of the novel is what the author is trying to say and prove.

What then is the theme of the story we began creating in the previous chapter? I think we would all agree that it is ambition. But frankly I think that one word is far too general to be of great use to the aspiring novelist. After all, many novels have the same theme. What, then, is the specific theme of the novel we were creating? What were we trying to say?

Putting it at its most basic, I would say that it is the story of a young girl's ambition to succeed in becoming an international skating star.

But is this enough to drive the story forward? Is it specific enough to determine not only the way the story is going to end, but what is going to happen in the novel which will lead logically and systematically to that end?

Very well! So we can now add to that storyline by saying that the theme of the novel is that the young girl's ambition to succeed *at all costs* eventually brings her to the realisation that ruthlessness brings its own rewards.

In other words, we have the twin themes of ambition and ruthlessness, and together they provide the drive that the story needs.

BUT WHAT THEMES ARE IMPORTANT TO TEENAGERS?

Refer back to the characteristics of adolescence we discussed in Chapter One and try to think of some. There is the coming to terms with innate sex drive for one; making, or the failure to make, adequate relationships is another. What about the challenging of authority in all its forms? And the determination to live one's own life? These are just some of many.

Assignment 4.

Examine the storyline you wrote briefly about at the end of Chapter Four. Decide what is the theme – or themes – of that basic storyline and ask yourself if it is likely to create sufficient conflict to drive the story forward.

VIEWPOINT.

It is safe to say that the most favoured viewpoint method used by writers of teenage novels is the first person viewpoint. Though this viewpoint method – where everything is seen through the eyes of the main character and is in the first person singular – has the disadvantage of lack of variety of characters and locations; nevertheless, because of the demands of the teenager for in-depth portrayal of the main character, with whom the reader identifies, this disadvantage can be disregarded. This is a logical extension of the importance of reader-identification. Just as Mills and Boon readers wish to identify with the main character in the novel, so the teenage reader wants to identify with the teenage girl. She wishes to suspend disbelief and live, in her mind, the life of the teenage girl she is reading about. She wishes to go through the agonies of indecision or betrayal or frustration the main character is suffering, because she herself has suffered those same agonies. And teenage girls – like their mothers – like to have a good cry at times. It is possible of course, as in Mills and Boon novels, for the third person viewpoint method to be used, but, as in those novels, the main character should be present in every scene in the book. It is, in other words, a first person story told in the third person singular where the viewpoint does not change at all throughout the book. Frankly, I find that being restricted to one viewpoint when I have only thirty or forty thousand words to play around with is no restriction at all. In fact, using more than one viewpoint would seriously weaken my novels since I would not be able to give sufficient attention to any of the characters involved.

Therefore, I believe that not only is it wise for reader-identification purposes to stick to one viewpoint character, but I also make – for exactly the same reason – that viewpoint character a teenage girl.

But which teenage girl? is the question you must ask yourself. After all, there will be more than one teenage girl in your novel.

The answer is simple. It must be the girl who has a problem to solve. In the story I have been constructing, the viewpoint character must be the girl whose ruthless ambition leads her into dire trouble – and who eventually learns from the tragic mistakes she makes.

Assignment 5.

Decide which of your characters is your viewpoint character. State briefly and clearly what her problems are and how you believe at this early planning stage her problems are going to be solved or resolved.

THE SETTINGS.

Having decided on the viewpoint character, it is time to consider the locations she lives in and the places she is likely to visit in the course of the story. Obviously, since she is of school age, school itself is going to play a part; so is her home, and so is her home town. It is therefore important to decide first, where the girl lives. Is it in a city, a town or a village? If it is a town or a city, which part does she live in? Is it a middle-class or working-class area? Is it near the sea or deep in the country? Does it have a large river running through it? Does it have a modern town centre as so many towns and cities have nowadays?

It is important to decide these matters right at the beginning of your planning stage, because locations and settings influence greatly the actions of your characters and therefore the plot of the story.

Assignment 6.

Decide where the main action of your story is going to take place. Give it a name; preferably a fictitious one but base the city, town or village on a place *you actually know*. In one of my novels, the location was Whitby – though I didn't refer to it by that name – and the reason I chose Whitby was simple: I had been on holiday there and thought the place had great character.

The next step is to draw, simple maps of locations – assuming as is likely your story will occur in more than one place. I put in the main places, such as the home, the school, the town centre – where so many teenagers hang around on a Saturday afternoon – the sports centre, the cafe and the youth club.

Assignment 7.

Draw a simple map of the town or city or village you have decided upon as the main location for your novel. Then construct one for each other location involved in your story. Remember to put in the places of importance to your characters.

Having done that, consider the other locations your main character is certain to visit in the course of the action of the story. For instance, in the story of the roller-skater, she is certain to visit the town where the regional or national competitions are going to be held. Consider also the places she is going to visit.

To begin with, her home. What kind of house is it? Terraced, detached or a semi? Of course, it could be a flat. Where in relation to the town is it? Is it on a hill, for example? If it is, what can she see from such a vantage-point?

What kind of school does she attend? Is it a grammar school? Or a modern comprehensive? Are there any playing fields on the campus? Is it in the centre of town or on the outskirts? Do your characters have to travel by school bus to get there?

All these factors affect the action of your novel so it is important to get a clear picture of them in your mind. I find that I have more confidence when it comes to the writing of the actual novel if I have done my 'homework' beforehand.

Assignment 8.

Describe clearly, with the aid of maps, diagrams and descriptions, the main places of interest, i.e. the youth club or cafe or disco hall, your characters are likely to visit in the course of the novel.

YOUR CHARACTERS.

By this time, you should have a very definite view of the characters who will inhabit your novel. Remember that the action of the novel should revolve around approximately six or seven characters. Let us therefore consider briefly at this stage the characters who will inhabit this make-believe world you are creating. Let us return once more to my initial idea of the girl with skating ambitions. We have the following characters:

1. *Julia Warner*, the viewpoint character, sixteen years old.

2. *Sue Warner*, her mother, who is 35 years old.

3. *John Warner*, her father, 40 years old.

4. *Keith Manning*, Julia's skating partner, 18 years old.

5. *Karen Wishart*, Julia's best friend, who is keen on:

6. *Perry Carter*, 18 years old, a newcomer to the club, formerly from London.

Here we have our six main characters around whom the

action of the novel will revolve, but of course other characters will also be introduced in the course of the story – some of the girls at school for instance and those she meets at the club, but these will be briefly sketched. You will notice that I have decided to make Karen keen on Perry because when he asks Julia to be his partner and she accepts, her action is going to cause even greater conflict for the simple fact that Karen is Julia's best friend. And as we all know, conflict is the essence of any good novel.

Assignment 9.

Make a list of your main characters – six or seven at the most – as though you are naming the cast of a play. State their names, relationships and ages. Look out for possible conflict situations that may arise between your characters and make a note of them.

In all probability, it was a character in a particular incident that gave you the initial idea regarding the kind of novel you have decided to write. Having decided on a theme or themes which hopefully will have clarified your aim in writing this particular novel, it is time to consider your characters in relation to it. I think it goes without saying that your choice of theme must inevitably influence your choice of characters. If one of your themes is ambition, then your main characters are going to be ambitious. Their actions are going to be the actions of ambitious characters – with all the inevitable conflicts that surround ambition. And we are going to see the effect that this driving force has on each of your characters. Remember that ambition can have good and bad effects, depending on the intensity with which and the degree to which your characters are prepared to go to achieve their aims. What they do not only affects their own lives, but that of others too.

So a novelist must choose his characters carefully to show both good and bad effects, otherwise the novel will be one-sided; and of course those characters must be clearly delineated and different from each other, not only to provide the essential variety but to avoid confusion in the minds of your readers.

Your novel is to be the story of the loves, hates, rivalries and conflicts that develop between your characters, so choose your characters carefully in order to create conflict.

CONFLICT.
It cannot be stressed enough that all novels must contain conflict of some kind and to some degree. Your theme must to some extent influence the conflict that exists within it. Consider two themes: loneliness and ambition.

In which of the two would you expect to find the greatest amount of external conflict?

I think I would be right in saying that ambition is the more likely. That is not to say that loneliness as a theme does not invite conflict, but it is more likely to be internal – within the mind of your main character – though not entirely of course. That internal conflict is sure to burst into external conflict at times, giving it depth and roundness which makes it live.

Assignment 10.

Decide what kind of conflicts MUST exist in your own novel; include both internal and external conflicts in your consideration. Write briefly what kind of conflict situations you consider your viewpoint character is likely to be involved in. Explain how those situations have arisen – they should have arisen out of the action and motivation of your character – and show how they affect other characters in your story.

I don't expect you to tie yourself down to the situations you have already invented, but I would expect that one dramatic situation would lead inexorably to another. You should find that this leads to the genesis of a complex plot – though in the case of the teenage novel, not too complex, or depth of characterisation will be sacrificed to the demands of a complicated plot.

YOUR INITIAL RESEARCH.
If, like me, you like to write about situations, procedures, events or locations about which you know next to nothing, it is essential to do some initial research before getting on to the actual plotting of your novel – though much of this will already be brewing in your mind. For instance, I know nothing about roller-skating as a serious pastime; in fact, the idea for a story dealing with that background came as a result of a television programme I saw. It excited me because it might be interesting to teenagers.

Since I knew nothing about roller-skating, I had to find out more about it before I could go on with the writing of the novel.

My first port of call was my local library where I asked if any books had been published on the subject. It happened they were unable to help but since it was obvious from the television programme that many of the movements and sequences were like those used in ice-skating, I borrowed books on that subject instead.

I also enquired if the local librarians – people who always seem to know what's going on in the neighbourhood – knew of any young people who were actually involved in the sport. They suggested I contact the manager of the local sports centre – which I did – and who proved able to help me. Though there were no local roller-skating clubs, he knew of one in the next town which I visited.

I then interviewed the people involved – teenagers as well as parents – and they provided me with a great deal of information as well as the problems which they had encountered over the years. I went armed with a reporters' notebook in which I had jotted down all the questions which I needed to ask – two to a page – and left room for others that would occur to me. I ALWAYS MAKE A POINT OF ASKING WHAT POSSIBLE CONFLICT SITUATIONS ARISE IN THE COURSE OF TRAINING AND COMPETING.

In this way, I was able to obtain a great deal of information which helped me in creating my plot. But I always kept accurate details of books I read, people I interviewed, their addresses and their phone numbers. I assumed that I would have to get in touch with them during the second and final drafts of my novel in order to verify facts I was not sure of.

THE PLOT OF YOUR NOVEL.
The plot of a novel can be described as the series of events and actions that propel the story forward. To put it simply, it is what HAPPENS in a story. And before we go any further I should emphasise once more that those events and actions should arise out of the natural actions and reactions of your characters. Plot must spring

67

naturally out of the thoughts and motives and desires of the characters you have created.

It is important to remember that every action has a reaction and that reaction will create another reaction; just like the chain-reaction of a nuclear explosion. Look at the actions of your characters in this light and for every action let there be a reaction so that the story is propelled forward to a conclusion that you have already decided upon. Though this should be said: that decision is only a temporary one; it can be changed if you think that a different ending would be better. After all, it is your novel, and you are in charge.

Assignment 11.

Begin to plot your novel by briefly describing in chronological order the events in which she is involved. As stated above, this list of events is a temporary one, designed only to get your mind working on cause and effect, action and reaction.

Let us now examine what you have already decided upon.

You have decided what your theme is.

You have decided who your viewpoint character is and who the other main characters are.

You have decided what kind of conflict situations they will be involved in.

You have made a temporary list of events in which your characters are involved – the genesis of your plot.

Notice that we still haven't decided at which point your

novel is going to begin; that will come later. You have completed a great deal of the preliminary work and should have a far better idea of your characters, plot and setting. You may want to start writing immediately. But resist that urge if you can. There are several more factors to consider – factors which could well modify your story. Jot your ideas down by all means; that is essential. Write about the situations that excite you if you must – but do wait until everything is complete before committing yourself finally.

So now to the next stage: characterisation.

6

CREATING BELIEVABLE CHARACTERS

If you really want to create believable characters, you have to believe in them yourself; it's as simple as that. But how do you create them? Easier said than done, you may say. That's what this chapter is about.

Initially, it is important that the viewpoint character you have in mind must be someone you like. It may be someone you know, a young girl on whom you are basing your character, or it may be someone you have created out of your own mind. Whichever one you use, it is important that she is a person you like. It is not important at this stage to have a clear, in-depth view of that girl; look upon her as someone you are meeting for the first time. And like someone you meet for the first time, you may feel you'd like to get to know her better – in other words, the chemistry is right; if it's someone you're wary of, forget her, because it is important, at this first meeting in the mind, that you like the girl whose story you are going to tell.

But be careful; liking is not enough. You must also understand her and be aware of her faults as well as her more admirable traits; you must see clearly, without bias, her weaknesses as well as her strengths. You must feel her happiness and excitement, her remorse and shame,

71

her fears and tribulations, her pangs of guilt, her feelings of delight and compassion. Only then will you create a true rounded character – one who will not appear like a cardboard figure against a flat background.

You can only do this successfully by getting inside your character to the extent of being that character, not only when you write about her but all the time you are preparing, thinking, and planning your novel.

In other words: YOU MUST BE THAT PERSON. You must experience the multitude of emotional contradictions and delights that make us what we are. You must know her even better than you know yourself.

Great! Tell me something new. Tell me how to do it.

Very well. Let's go back to Julia Warner. When I first thought of her and the situation she found herself in, my first impression was that she was a happy pleasant girl about sixteen years old, determined in her ambition to succeed as a skater, and yet friendly and outgoing; the kind of girl who would have many friends of both sexes. Since she was to be my heroine, and since this ambition of hers was to create problems for her, I had to make her a person with whom the readership would and could identify. Any failings she had would have to be more than counterbalanced by her good points, and those failings would be the result of folly arising from immaturity rather than sheer malice and selfishness.

In other words, I knew from the very beginning when I'd thought about the theme and situation, that she was going to be the kind of person I would like. If I didn't feel that way about her, then I would find it difficult to have sympathy or empathy with her – and that would mean that I could not possible *be* Julia while I was writing about her and the novel would have failed right from the start.

So now I know in a cursory fashion what sort of person she is like: foolish rather than vindictive; sinned against rather than sinning.

Assignment 12.

Write down briefly what kind of person your main character is going to be. There is no need to go into detail yet; that will come later. Between twenty-five and fifty words will be enough.

The next thing I had to consider is her appearance. I tried to visualise Julia in my mind, doing the thing she liked most: skating. I saw her in the hall of the sports centre while she was in the middle of her training session. She was about five foot four inches tall, slim and athletic, with slender legs and she skated with grace and confidence. Her hair was long and fair and tied in a pony tail which trailed behind her as she whirled across the floor. As she came closer and stopped in front of me, I saw she had a fresh healthy complexion, blue almond-shaped eyes, a wide mouth – and the smile she gave revealed a set of almost perfect white teeth. As a matter of fact, the only thing that marred them was the tiny chip off one of her incisors – the result of a tumble she received while training a few years earlier. I could tell that given a few years, she was going to be a very attractive woman. And yet, I detected a certain lack of confidence which came over when I noticed a slight flicker in her eyes. It was not there for long, but it told me that Julia was still struggling to achieve maturity.

Can you now see what I'm doing?

In my mind, I am meeting this girl, getting to see her, even know her psychologically. But more of that later.

Assignment 13.

Answer the following questions about your own main character and build up a more extensive profile on her.

1. How tall is she?

2. What is her weight?

3. Is she fat, thin or just right for her age and height?

4. What is her health like?

5. How physically fit is she?

6. What is her eyesight like, and if it is poor, does she wear spectacles?

7. What colour is her hair?

8. What is its texture? Coarse or fine? Thick or thin?

9. Has it been styled?

10. What is the shape and complexion of her face?

11. What are the colour and shape of her eyes?

12. What kind of mouth and lips has she got?

13. Are her teeth regular and white? Describe them.

14. Has she any distinctive scars or blemishes?

15. Has she any mannerisms which might give you an indication of her character?

By now you should have a much clearer view of your character's physical characteristics; you should be able to see her right in front of you if you close your eyes. But also, and in some ways even more important, you should be getting an idea of her personality as well.

Back to Julia again.

When I thought of her in that sports centre and saw her skating, I also saw two other people standing there, anxiously and critically watching her performance: her parents. I realised that since most teenage novels are concerned with relationship problems, particularly those between adolescent and parents, it was important to examine in depth the kind of home Julia came from and the kind of parents she had.

I decided to make Julia's parents lower middle-class and ambitious for her. So it was important for me to consider her mother and father and the influence they had on her. I had to decide to make the father either a self-employed man or the manager of the local Sports Centre. Being a self-employed man would give him relative freedom to travel the country with Julia to various competitions; on the other hand, making him the manager of the Sports Centre would give him the freedom of allowing his daughter to practise out of hours. We have all heard stories of swimmers who have fathers in charge of swimming pools.

Eventually, I made him the manager of the Sports Centre, but decided, since skating is an expensive sport, to make the mother the proprietress of a small boutique in the centre of town. Being her own boss would give Mrs Warner the freedom to travel too, especially if she had a friend who would manage the shop in her absence. Notice that I now have another character – a minor one admittedly – who comes on to the scene purely for the purposes of plotting.

I then had to ask myself the question: why were the parents, Sue and John Warner, so keen to support Julia's ambition? The answer was simple; they had once been skaters themselves before getting married and deciding to leave London to live in East Anglia. Incidentally, my research divulged the fact that there is an excellent roller-skating rink at Bury St Edmunds – which, as you know, is a small town in East Anglia. I may well use that rink in my story, since competitions are often held there.

But let's get back to the parents.

I had to consider their ages, their temperaments, physique, marriage, enthusiasms and friends as well as aspects of their past lives which had a bearing on the story. So I decided that John was forty; Sue thirty-six. They had a happy stable marriage which was based on trust and this happiness spilled over into their attitude to Julia and, more important still, into her attitude to them. They were both ambitious athletic people, outgoing and gregarious. She was not the stay-at-home type of mother; she was a person in her own right who had established a flourishing business in East Parham, the town where they live. She had a friend, Edna, who worked for her and whom she could trust to carry on the business in her absence.

In addition to this, I had to consider where in East Parham the family lived and if they had any decided views, for example on religion, education and work. Were there any grandparents still alive? Any aunts, uncles and cousins with whom they had close connections? And if so, where did they live? Had Julia any brothers and sisters? For the sake of the story, I decided that Julia was an only child; a younger brother or sister would have created complications on the plotting. I decided – though this might not be revealed – that because Julia's was a difficult birth, her mother decided to limit her family and concentrate instead on starting a business.

It may not seem important, but I believe it is essential

to create a real living family with real mores and opinions. It is an important part of the background in which Julia has grown and developed. Were the problem to involve a family dispute of some sort which was central to the problem that Julia was facing, then I might well have decided to give her several brothers and sisters – a situation which would have added variety and complication to the story. I also like to create a family tree at this stage, though in the case of Julia this is not really important since hers is a nuclear family; the relationships are easy to remember since they involve only the father, mother and daughter.

I also consider at this stage the effect of this family situation on Julia. An only child has the best of everything, mother and father often dote on her, sometimes with disastrous consequences. But I discarded this possibility for the simple fact that that was another story and one I didn't want to consider while planning Julia's story. So I decided to give her parents a very sensible attitude towards their only child; I decided that Julia was not going to be spoilt; she was expected to help out in the home, often getting meals ready for her parents when she arrived home from school.

All these factors must be considered when building up a character because they have a direct bearing on each character's psychological make-up, which is the next aspect we must consider. But first:

Assignment 14.

Consider, with regard to your own main character, the aspect of the immediate family and its effect on that character.

77

Ask yourself the following questions:

1. What are the names and ages of the parents?

2. What are their occupations?

3. How many children are there in the family? If there are several, state their names, ages and the position of your main character in that family; that is, was your main character the first, second, third born. It does have a very real effect on the way your main character has been reared.

4. To what social class does your family belong?

5. Where do they live and what kind of house do they own?

6. Are the grandparents still alive and where do they live? Remember, a grandmother may often be a mother-confessor figure and play an important role in the emotional life and development of your main character – and therefore influence your plotting.

7. Is the family a nuclear or extended one? If extended, are there any uncles, aunts and cousins who live in the same area?

8. Who are the family friends? Do they have any children of the same age as your main character – and if so, what is their relationship to one another?

9. How alike to her parents is your main character? Has she inherited any specific characteristics? For instance, though she may look like her mother, she may have her father's temperament.

All these factors have an important relationship to a person's emotional make-up. When considering Julia's character and the emotional factors which influence it, I first had to decide whether she was an introvert or an extrovert or something in between. I decided that because she was a sportswoman she had to be mainly extroverted – though not excessively so – and yet I felt that since she had artistic leanings (her love of graceful movement), there had also to be some introversion. This is not unusual when you think of it; we all fluctuate between extroversion and introversion and it often depends on the situations in which we find ourselves. In other words, we all play out the roles we are expected to at various times. Julia's introversion, I decided, had to reveal itself when she was alone – or during a 'confessional' with her mother or best friend.

Deciding on her ambition, of course, was a simple matter; what wasn't so simple was the portrayal of the extent of that ambition and the effect of her relative immaturity on that ambition. I had to consider at this stage any fantasies she might possess. They naturally concerned her ambition and were closely linked. She fantasised about becoming a champion and that in turn fuelled her ambitious determination to succeed. I also had to consider if fantasy, ambition and determination could lead to obsession – and the effect that would have on her relationships.

I felt that there was a danger that Julia could well become thoughtless – to say the least – if she allowed these factors to dominate her life; and for a time, they do. But on the other side of the scale, I had also to give her the ideals of fair play, sportsmanship in its widest sense, the effect of her upbringing and the ideas of good and bad which had been inculcated in her. I knew that, since I was seeking possible conflict situations, Julia would create problems not only for herself but also for people around her, and that despite her attempts at rationalisation (convincing herself that taking her friend's skating partner was permissible, for instance), she did experience moments of guilt. Important for the lessons – her insight into herself – that she learns at the end of the story.

You will notice that some aspects of the plot are already beginning to manifest themselves.

So what about your own character?

Assignment 15.

Answer the following questions:

1. Is your character an extrovert, an introvert, or a mixture of both?

2. Does she have any fantasies and ambitions which may affect her and the story you are going to tell?

3. Do these fantasies and ambitions spill over into obsessive behaviour and, if so, how does it affect your story?

4. Does she have any ideals – ideas of good and bad, fairness or unfairness – which have been inculcated by her parents in the course of her upbringing?

5. Do any of these attributes suggest any conflict situations in which your character could find herself AS A RESULT OF HER OWN ACTIONS? If so, make a list of them.

This leads naturally to a consideration of the emotional

factors which influence a person's life. Among the first things I had to consider when building up Julia's character were her strengths and weaknesses. Obviously, she has to be a strong person physically, but it was the psychological and emotional factors that interested me more. Her strength was that determination to succeed, her ambition to become a skating star, and yet ironically, taken to extremes, this strength became a weakness which created problems for her. I had to consider also the people she likes and dislikes. Were there any boys or girls she got on well with – or otherwise? I had to consider her attitude to the opposite sex; to her parents – as well as all the other people with whom she came into contact. And of course what possible conflict situations could arise in the course of those encounters? How persistent was she? Obviously very persistent, though this persistence does cause moments of despair. These moments of doubt were important to the story; recall your own adolescent days and the often mortifying moments of doubt and despair you experienced. I also decided to make her a fun-loving individual who likes to fight hard as well as play hard. This facet of her character was important because in teenage fiction, the readership likes both action and humour. I had to decide that most of the time she was emotionally self-sufficient, though obviously there would be times when self-doubt would set in. Because of her commitment to sport, I decided that she found it easy to make friends and form attachments, the more so because when she betrays her best friend, that friend as well as all the others is prepared to forgive and forget because she realises it was an aberration. And of course, guilt had to play a big part in her eventual coming-to-terms with her behaviour – though obviously not to the extent of being self-destructive. All these factors played a big part in deciding the course of the novel.

Assignment 16.

Answer the following questions about your character's emotional make-up.

1. What are her strengths and weaknesses?

2. Does she have any particular hopes and fears – and what are they?

3. Has she any special loves and hates of people, places, food, things?

4. Is she patient, suffering fools gladly – or does she possess a temper?

5. What is her approach like to work and play, particularly when it comes to her favourite occupation?

6. What are her relationships like with members of her own as well as the opposite sex?

7. Is she carefree or fastidious? Think of her bedroom and the way she looks after it.

8. Has she any inferiority or superiority feelings, and how far is overconfidence a ploy to hide feelings of inferiority?

9. How emotionally self-sufficient is she and how easy or difficult does she find it to make permanent attachments?

10. Have you, in the course of answering these

questions, discovered any possible areas of conflict which can be utilised in planning your novel? If so, make a list of them; if you don't you may forget them.

By now, you should have created a living, rounded character. You should love and understand her – and sympathise with her when through her own folly, she finds herself in serious trouble.

You should create a similar profile for every main character in your novel, note their relationships and the way they are going to inter-react. THOSE INTER-REACTIONS SHOULD HOPEFULLY CREATE A LOGICAL PLOT.

7

FROM CHARACTER TO PLOT

Let me first repeat my concept of a plot: it is the series of sequential events and actions that propel the story forward to its logical conclusion. To put it simply, it is what HAPPENS in a story. And before we go any further I should emphasise once more that those events and actions should arise out of the natural actions and reactions of your characters. Plot must spring naturally out of the thoughts and motives and desires and actions of the characters you have created.

It is important to remember that every action has a reaction and that reaction will create another reaction. Look at the actions of your characters in this light and for every action let there be a reaction so that the story is propelled forward to its inevitable conclusion – a conclusion, remember, that you have already decided upon. After all, it is your novel, and you are in charge and if you have chosen your character wisely and those characters act IN CHARACTER, then you should have no trouble in constructing an interesting and exciting plot.

Let us remember that though characters are sometimes subservient to plot in a short story, particularly one with a twist ending, it is essential in a novel that character takes pride of place. If you have created the right character to illustrate the theme you have chosen, that character will dictate the plot. That is to say, she will act and react to each particular situation in such a way that the story will flow naturally and logically to its conclusion. If for some reason it does not work, if you feel instinctively that something is wrong, then you may have created the wrong character for the job. You may discover that the character you have created will not behave in the way you want her to, and if you force that character to do something that is against her will, then the action and the ending will be contrived. That sounds as if a character has a personality of her own that transcends that of the novelist and that he has lost control of her. In some respects, that is true; a character does have a personality – it is the one the novelist created for her. But it must always be the novelist's character, dancing to the novelist's tune. That tune is the theme and if that character will not do the novelist's bidding, it is not a good situation for that novelist to find himself or herself in. THE NOVELIST SHOULD ALWAYS BE IN CONTROL.

Of course, it may well happen that you prefer the plot the character dictates; it may be far better than the original, with more emotion, more conflict, more suspense, and more chance of a successful sale. If so, then write it that way. Go back and revise your characterisation and plot, but be in charge.

Let me explain what I mean by the maxim that 'character must create plot'.

Imagine this character, in this situation, with this problem:

Emma is sixteen, comes from a home with a domineering father who though he loves his daughter is so protective that he will not give her the freedom she wants and needs. Her mother is in awe of Emma's father and agrees with everything he says. Emma decides to tell her parents that she is going to a disco one Saturday night and will not be home until the early hours of Sunday morning. Moreover, she is going with Steve, a guy who is not very responsible and whom her parents don't approve of – particularly as he rides a motorcycle and wears outlandish gear.

A common enough situation, you might say; and I would agree with you.

But Emma has grown up to be as wilful as her father – and is determined to have her own way. It's my life, she says, and I'll live it my way.

A potentially explosive situation.

Let us start where Emma comes home from school one Friday evening and enters the living room where her father is reading the newspaper, having experienced a particularly difficult day at work. He is glad to put his feet up for the weekend.

Emma anticipates trouble and as a result is uptight. When she tells her parents that she is going out to the disco the following night, she announces it rather more aggressively than she intends. Her father is annoyed at being told not asked and tells her that she may go only if he comes to get her.

That annoys Emma and she tells him she's old enough to look after herself – again rather truculently – and besides, Phil will be bringing her home. It is at this point that she tells them that it will be after midnight.

The time of return as well as her choice of escort angers her father more and he delivers an order: she is not to go to the disco.

That makes Emma even more determined to do her own thing – and she announces firmly that she is going and that nothing is going to stop her.

Furious at being spoken to in such a disrespectful way,

her father grabs hold of her shoulders and shakes her. Emma, now in tears, loses control of herself and lashes out with her foot, striking her father on his shin. He in turn lashes out with his hand and strikes her across the face.

Emma rushes out of the house and seeks refuge at Steve's flat; he offers to let her stay the night.

I shall stop there, but can you see what a dangerous situation Emma is landing herself in? And all because of her character, which is so much like her father's. Can you imagine what is going to happen after that?

Now let us keep the names, the location and the problem, but change the characters. Let us make Emma rather a sensible girl – very much like her mother perhaps – and let us make her father less domineering though just as caring for her safety.

Emma arrives home on the Friday afternoon to find her father reading his newspaper in the living room. Nervously, Emma *asks* her parents if they mind her going to the disco with Steve the following night. Her parents like Steve, who is a boy they can trust, but even so they are doubtful – especially when she tells them diffidently that it is a special disco which goes on until the early hours of Sunday morning.

Her father is gentle but firm. She cannot go. But Emma is hurt, knowing that since all her friends will be there, she will be humiliated. She rushes upstairs in tears.

A few minutes later, her mother comes up to tell her that she and Emma's father have been discussing the problem and now he agrees that she may go. On one condition. That he picks her and Steve up from the disco when it ends.

Reluctantly, Emma agrees.

Can you now see how the plot changes when the characters change?

However, we still haven't decided at which point your novel is going to begin: that time has arrived.

At this stage, you have done all the preparatory work which is so essential before you start writing, and it is now the time to get down to work. You have examined the theme of your novel, made your characters live, and in the process created a convincing, feasible plot without any contrivances and loose ends.

You should start your novel at or near a point of change in your main character's life.

AT OR NEAR A POINT OF CHANGE.

Remember that. It will help to crystallise your mind in preparation for the task you have set yourself.

But changes can be both physical and emotional. In Julia's case, there was the physical change in that she had to choose a new partner when Keith sustained his accident, but there was an emotional aspect to that change: there were her feelings of loss at losing Keith as well as feelings of guilt at taking Karen's partner away from her. It was a change which was going to cause a great deal of conflict and provide the impetus to drive the story forward to an inevitable yet not wholly predictable end. Remember this: it is best if you can combine both physical and emotional changes at the start of your novel.

Assignment 17.

Examine your own story carefully and decide where the point of change comes in your main character's life. Write it down in about twenty-five words so that you will have a clear idea where to start. Try to make that change both physical and emotional.

After examining Julia's story carefully, I saw that starting at that point was going to create problems: I was going to be forced to handle a great deal of retrospect which is always a difficult thing to do, and at the same time, I had to introduce my main characters, set the scene and give a very strong hint of the problem to come. I had to decide what the functions of a first chapter were.

To begin with, I had to introduce the main characters – Julia, her partner Keith, her best friend Karen, and her parents.

Secondly, I had to set the scene. I could have started at Julia's home, prior to going to the Sports Centre to practise and bring out there some of the anxiety about the forthcoming competition. I decided against it not only because it lacked immediacy; it did not tell us that the story was about roller-skating, and it lacked action and drama. It gave me little opportunity to show Julia or the other characters against a backdrop which was so important to all of them.

It is important therefore to choose the right scene.

Assignment 18.

Decide the scene or location which best prepares your readers for the kind of story they are going to read. Remember that most readers always glance at the first few paragraphs before deciding to buy. Be sure therefore to make it a potentially exciting one. And above all, remember it must be one in which the other main characters can be present and which will adequately introduce them too.

So let's go on.

Thirdly, I had to bring out conflict. I decided that Keith's accident would provide both external and internal conflict and that where he fell was by far the most dramatic place to start.

Fourthly, I had to state the problem which was: how were they going to compete together if Keith was injured? Again, it was obvious that the moment of injury was the best time for this to be stated.

Fifthly, I had to create the mood: and the mood of this story is the excitement of the competition and of preparing for it. Again the moment of the accident seemed the right place to start.

As a matter of fact, I decided to start a few minutes before the accident because in doing so I was able to comply with all the requirements of the first chapter.

It is evening and Julia and Keith are practising at the Sports Centre. Present are her parents who are coaching them, as well as her best friend, Karen. Her parents warn them that with a competition approaching, they must not take any unnecessary risks or they won't be able to compete. The thought chills Julia – and minutes later, she stumbles. But it is Keith who falls heavily and is hurt.

In this way, I have (a) introduced the main characters, (b) set the scene, (c) introduced an element of conflict, (d) stated the problem, and (e) set the mood.

Assignment 19.

Decide what the first scene of your novel is going to be. Describe it briefly as I have done above, trying to comply with the requirements of a first chapter.

Now that I know where I am to begin, I can start

planning the whole novel by breaking it down into scenes. I do this initially in a brief and casual manner. I take some large sheets of lined paper and begin to number the scenes and describe the action of the novel in a sequential way. For example:

1. Julia Warner is at the Sports Centre, practising with her partner, Keith Manning. Her mother and father are present, watching and coaching, while her best friend, Karen Wishart, who is also a keen roller-skater, lends her moral support. That night, a newcomer arrives: Perry Carter, who informs them that he too is keen on skating and shows off his expertise by dancing with Karen. Julia is sure she has seen him before.

2. After the practice session, Julia, Keith, Karen and Perry go to a coffee bar where Perry boasts that he is a champion. Keith takes an instant dislike to him, but Julia and Karen are prepared to excuse his boastful behaviour.

3. Keith walks Julia home and confesses that he is sure that Perry is going to be trouble.

4. That night in the solitude of her bedroom, Julia recalls the expert way Perry skated – and realises that he is better than Keith and that with him as a partner, she could go far. But that would mean abandoning Keith. She dismisses the idea – but the seed has nevertheless been planted.

I go on in this sequential fashion until I reach the end of the story. If my plotting is right, I should have created approximately twenty scenes, each one leading inexorably to the next and each one containing the essential conflict and suspense which drives the story forward to its inevitable conclusion. Having done this, I then revise by asking myself if the sequence of events is logical, and if there is sufficient conflict. I ask myself too if there is any way I can improve the story by creating additional conflict, and if there is sufficient conflict in each scene to sustain between 1,500 and 2,000 words.

Assignment 20.

Break down your own story into scenes, until you have created approximately twenty scenes in all, though at the same time being aware that you may well have to change them. This awareness is important; it will create in you the knowledge that this is a preliminary exercise and that you may alter it if you are not satisfied.

NOW YOU HAVE A MORE DETAILED PLOT AND YOU ARE ABOUT TO START. BUT FIRST WE MUST TRY TO CONVINCE YOUR PUBLISHER THAT YOU HAVE CREATED A SALEABLE PRODUCT.

8

CONVINCING YOUR EDITOR

You can do this in one of two ways: you can either write the whole novel and submit it to your publisher, or you can write a synopsis and first chapter and submit that. Submitting the whole novel, particularly for a newcomer to writing, has the advantage of the author's knowing the story he will write as well as giving to the editor of a particular series a complete work which he or she may accept, reject or ask you to re-write. On the other hand, a synopsis and first chapter has the advantage of saving the author a great deal of work, since, if the idea does not fit in with the requirements of a particular series, then the author is informed before he writes that the work will be unacceptable and that allows him to seek another publisher. Of course, he may be told what those requirements are in which case they may help him in the revision and subsequent submission of a revised synopsis, or, alternatively, assist him when he plans another novel for that publisher. This is part of market research and the information gained is invaluable. It will provide the author with knowledge of the range of themes and plots that a series expects.

However, to many writers, the concept of a synopsis strikes fear into their very souls. What is a synopsis? they ask. What does an editor expect from a synopsis? How do I set about writing one?

The function of this chapter is to answer those questions and help you create a synopsis that will satisfy an editor.

But first let's look at further pros and cons of writing a synopsis.

Many writers I know actually shy away from writing a detailed synopsis, preferring rather to give an indication – although a pretty good one – of the idea of the novel that is fermenting in their brains. They feel that too detailed a synopsis would curb the excitement they get when they actually write the novel and perhaps curb also the spontaneity which they consider essential. They fear that the novel will become stilted and lack that essential sparkle. I know that Iris Gower, the Swansea novelist, who is published by Century Hutchinson, prefers to write a brief synopsis; indeed for her, a synopsis of under 2,000 words was sufficient to write six novels, each one 150,000 words long; it was sufficient for her publishers too – because she already had a 'track record' with them and presumably they were confident she was able to produce the goods. As indeed, she was. Another highly successful novelist I know can only write a synopsis AFTER she has completed the novel and that synopsis was included with the completed novel when it was despatched to her editor. It gave that editor an excellent idea of what to expect when she read the manuscript.

Frankly, I don't work like that. I prefer to write such a detailed synopsis that when it is finished, so too is the novel. All I need to do is to write it. That sounds rather cynical, I know, but it isn't really. That detailed synopsis gives me a certain confidence; I know the setting, I know the characters, I know the conflicts that exist between them, and I know the plot is sufficiently complicated to get me from A to Z. In other words, I know that I will be able to write that novel. I also know that if an editor commissions me, then I have no fears that I won't be able to complete it. After all, it would be devastating to my morale to be commissioned to write a novel and discover halfway through that I could not for some reason – say, that the plotting was deficient in that it lacked sufficient conflict and suspense – complete it. What an indignity that would be!

As I've stated earlier, there is another advantage to writing a detailed synopsis: it gives your publisher a thorough knowledge of the book you intend writing and therefore whether it will fit their requirements. But that could also be a disadvantage. If your descriptions of the characters, settings and plot were not sufficiently exciting or romantic or adventurous – depending on the kind of novel the publishers were looking for – if it did not fit the requirements, it would come back with a negative reply.

Therefore, your synopsis should sell itself; it is up to you to show how exciting your novel is going to be – and how it's going to become a best seller!

So what should a synopsis contain? As a matter of fact, if you have carried out all the assignments I've given you in this book, then you have amassed all the information required. All you have to do is refer back to your answers and write the synopsis according to the following plan.

1. It should start with a statement of what the novel is about. Ideally, it should start with the name of your viewpoint character, her age and where she lives and give details of her family and friends. It should tell of her past life, and of the problem facing her and the reasons for

that problem manifesting itself at that particular time in her life. It should give a clear indication of the theme and of the way the novel is going to develop.

2. It should give information about the locations as well as the time in which it takes place. It should state where your main character lives – whether in the country or in a town or city or near the sea. It should also explain, if the main character moves away from home, the location she visits. It is well to have a clear idea in your own mind of the kind of place she lives in or visits and therefore it is wise to place the action in locations you know well. You may of course change the locations slightly and alter the names if you wish.

3. It should contain thorough information about your characters – particularly your main ones – and explain the conflicts that exist between them. (Remember that conflict is the essence of your novel.) This is the main part of your synopsis and much thought should go into it. Describe your characters clearly: physically, intellectually, mentally, and emotionally. You should know your characters even better than you know yourself; they should become real to you – to come alive so that you can actually hear them talk and see them act. This is vitally important because this is the point when your plot begins to take shape; remember that your characters should dictate the plot.

4. It should state where the story is going to begin, and of course it should always begin with your main character, preferably at a time of crisis, show the scene and state the problem facing him or her. You will also bring in your other main characters at this point and give more detailed information about their relationships with each

other and of the conflicts that exist between them, including of course reasons for those conflicts.

5. It should tell the editor what the plot is; that is, it should contain the sequence of events in as detailed a form as you can possibly manage. You will probably find at this stage that you are eager to start writing your novel – and if you feel that way, then perhaps you should. Frankly, I don't. My synopsis will take many drafts before it is finalised; before I am satisfied that it will convince my editor that she should let me write the story.

6. It should state where the story is going to end and how the problem facing your main character is resolved.

As I said earlier, my synopsis goes into several drafts, sometimes as many as six or seven. I start at the beginning and work my way through as quickly as I can; the first draft is done quickly so that I get down the excitement that I always get when an idea strikes me. I type or print it out, read it and edit it, adding as I go along. Then I repeat the operation, altering the story if it needs altering (this is where my characters dictate the plot) and ironing out any anomalies that may exist – and believe me they do exist. I must admit that working on a word processor makes my job much simpler and less arduous than using a steam typewriter. The first draft may only be five hundred words long; the second a thousand, but the final one may be three or four thousand words long. By the time I've reached that stage the novel is virtually written. All I have to do is break it into chapters, start writing and let my characters do the rest.

Assuming of course that I've convinced my editor that she should like the story – and I've agreed with any alterations she may have suggested. Incidentally, I usually agree with my editor; she knows what she wants and since she is impartial, she can be objective about my proposed novel and offer invaluable advice regarding its improvement.

9

GETTING DOWN TO WORK

At this stage, you will have done all the preparatory work which is so essential before you start writing, and it is now the time to get down to work. (Who had the temerity to suggest you haven't been working?) You have examined the theme of your novel, made your characters live, and in the process created a convincing, feasible plot without any contrivances and loose ends; you have decided at which point to start your story. But it is still not time to start writing; do I hear groans? Now you have to plan the structure of the novel; in other words, work out the chaptering.

As I've just said, much of the work has already been done. In Assignment 20, you broke down the action of your story into approximately twenty scenes; these scenes will be your chapters.

At this stage, I re-examine my scenes and decide (1) if the sequence is right, (2) if there are any scenes I have left out which are essential to the plot – If there are I write them in. (3) I ask myself if there is sufficient action and conflict in each scene for it to exist in its own right, remembering that every chapter must also advance the action and reveal facets of character.

When I am satisfied with the 'movement' of the story, I take a large A3 sheet of paper and block it into twenty numbered rectangles. Each one will contain a brief description of each scene, but this is written in pencil so that alterations may be made. You will notice that I still allow for changes to be made. I consider it important to alter the scenes – and their order, if necessary – if I think that it will create a better story.

I pin the plan on to the wall in front of my desk together with a list of the characters, their relationship to each other and a brief description of each; (it is surprisingly easy to give a character brown eyes at the beginning and blue eyes at the end; this eliminates that possibility.) I also pin up any maps of the locations I have made. These are to be my guides in the writing of the novel, making sure I don't make any blatant or ridiculous mistakes.

Alternatively, I write each scene on index cards; this gives me the advantage of flexibility since I am able to change the order of the scenes if I so wish. The disadvantage is obvious; I am unable to place them in full view as I am typing and therefore instant consultation of my plan – something I find invaluable – is not available to me.

My next step is to write a detailed description of each scene; this is my day-to-day working model. I usually use either a ring file or a spiral notepad and write each scene on a separate page. (Sometimes I may have to go on to a second page.) Based on the block plan, it is a description of each chapter and holds the following information:

1. The characters in the scene,

2. The location of the scene,

3. The reason why the characters are there,

4. The action of each character and their reactions to each other,

102

5. The time of day in which the action takes place.

I start always with the characters; for example: Julia is skating with Keith in the gymnasium of the local Sports Centre, watched anxiously and critically by her mother, Sue Warner, and her father, John Warner. Present also is her best friend, Karen Wishart. As Julia and Keith approach the area of the gymnasium where the viewers are seated on a bench, Julia stumbles and falls. Her mother rushes to her aid, warning her to be careful; she has only a few weeks to go before a very important competition. It is the first hint of possible trouble to come.

I go on in this fashion until I have sketched out the action of the chapter. I use no dialogue at all at this stage, but I often write down the actual ending of the scene, which is usually a cliff-hanger of some kind, or alternatively, end with a note of contradiction or hint of mystery.

Assignment 21.

Describe in some detail the characters, location and action of your First Scene as described above. Remember to refer back to the functions of a first chapter. State at which point the scene is going to end.

My next step is to work out a detailed description of each scene or chapter, taking care to include as much conflict as the scene can reasonably be expected to contain – too much can sometimes be counterproductive. Sometimes I have to combine two scenes to make one chapter. Once I have finished, I know with reasonable conviction that I can and will complete the novel, though

I will also know that there are some scenes which will be weak. At this stage, I don't worry unduly, though I must admit that I will search for some action, conflict or character which will strengthen not only the weak scenes but other connected scenes as well. However, if I can't think of some strategy immediately, I will not allow it to inhibit my writing of the novel. There is time for alteration later – during the revision and editing of the first draft.

Assignment 22.

Work out the action of EVERY SUBSEQUENT SCENE, stating clearly in each one, who is present, where the action takes place and the characters' reactions to the conflict that is present.

When I have completed this, I'm ready to work. So on with the writing of the first draft.

I spend the first half hour or so reading the chapter synopsis of the scene I'm going to write until I have established firmly in my mind exactly what it is I am trying to achieve; when the characters begin reacting to the situations in which they find themselves and start 'talking' to me, then, and only then, do I write. This is creativity at its most exciting and satisfying. When that happens, I find that my writing flows and in the course of about two hours or so, I have completed my first chapter.

I find it works not to expect near-perfection in my first draft; I assume and expect to do major revision at some time and therefore concentrate on getting the story down in black and white. Then I have something to work on. I never revise a chapter until I have completed the novel and in the writing of the first draft I concentrate only on the characters, their reactions and their dialogue. The settings I introduce in a most rudimentary form if I am not sure of their descriptions at the time; that the story flows is my paramount consideration. Detailed descriptions I leave until the second draft. After all, as Shakespeare said, 'The play's the thing!', so forget your conscience about it not being quite right, and get on with the action. Though having said that, I think it only fair to remind you that this is my method of working; you may prefer to work differently – and should do so if that is what works for you.

Once I have completed the whole novel, I put it aside for a week or so – other novelists leave their work for far longer before revising – and get on with something else, usually the planning and researching of another novel. The reason for this strategy is simple. Up until then, I have been too close to my work and am unable to judge it objectively. Taking a break away from it, enables me to approach it with a freshness which is essential to the critical reading and revision of the first draft.

Which brings me to the next step in the process of writing a novel.

10

WRITING THE SECOND DRAFT

In my first draft, I explored life with my characters and thoroughly enjoyed myself. Now it is time for the really hard work to begin. Strangely, this is the part I like best; it is the time when I put my critical faculties to work, knowing that I have written the whole novel, albeit in a most rudimentary form, yet aware that there is still much to do. Nevertheless, I have something in black and white, something concrete to work upon. I remember going to my first conference ever and hearing one of the main speakers say those very words; I didn't at the time understand, let alone appreciate, exactly what she meant. But with several novels under my belt and many short stories published, I am able to repeat her words, knowing from experience that her words were so true. This is the part where I make everything slot into place.

My first step as I stated in the previous chapter is to put my work aside for a short time – some authors prefer to put their work aside for months if they can – but speaking for myself, I prefer a few days, certainly not more than two weeks. Then I read the whole novel, making mental notes – and the occasional scribbled sentence or two – asking myself if the story flows and if the characters are acting in character and enquiring WHAT IS WRONG WITH IT. Notice that I set out with the assumption that there is something wrong; that the novel is, at this stage, far from ready to send to an editor. This I believe to be essential if you are not to have a rosy-spectacled view of your work and will help you when you shudder with embarrassment and despair at the horrible novel you have just written. Believe me, that will happen. You will ask yourself: Did I write this nonsense? and your immediate reaction will be to deposit the whole manuscript into the nearest bin.

Resist the temptation. Remind yourself that you have put a lot of work into the creation of this manuscript; it is your 'baby' and you are not going to throw it all away.

You now have something solid to work on. Ask yourself: O.K. So what's right with it? You will probably find much that is right – and that will give you confidence.

And having ascertained all these things, ask yourself: So how do I improve it?

The first thing I ask myself is: *would the reader identify herself with my main character*? Is she the sort of person the reader can sympathise with? Do her bad points counterbalance her good points?

I have found on occasion that because I understand my character so well, I write in certain actions which are credible to me, but because of the girl's psychological state at the time, her actions may appear rather hard and uncompromising. Adolescents often appear in that light, don't they? If that is the case, then usually I find that I haven't explained WHY the girl is reacting in that way – and the solution to the problem is simply to EXPLAIN her reactions. Then the reader understands and is able to sympathise with her.

The second question I ask is: *is there sufficient conflict, emotion and suspense in the story*? Normally, I find as I read the story that I will discover ways of improving it by creating more conflict, emotion and suspense. At this stage, I examine the story in its entirety, making short notes and suggesting how these faults may be improved – which I find is usually done by improving my characterisation.

The third question is: *do all the characters act and react in character?* If not, I make sure at this stage that they do and that means I examine closely and critically those actions and reactions.

The fourth thing I ask is: *are all the crises in ascending order of dramatic importance?* Is there a dark scene where all appears lost? And does the Seventh Cavalry come to the rescue? After all, there has to be a satisfactory resolution of the heroine's problem.

The fifth thing I ask is: *has it any humorous situations which will lighten the drama and the conflict?* If not, then I look through the whole plot and decide WHERE that humour is needed and then try to find something that fits in naturally with the action, yet will create a laugh. This, I must confess, is sometimes difficult. I found one of my novels rather too heavy and depressing at one point, so I felt I had to find a humorous situation which would make the reader laugh.

It was my daughter who came to the rescue. She was seventeen at the time and regularly attending the local Saturday disco in a foursome. I had gone to bed long before she arrived home, but next morning, she laughingly complained of the outrageous treatment she and her friend had suffered at the hands of the two young men who had escorted them home.

'My feet were killing me, dad,' she said. 'So Sue and I told Steve and Richard that if they were gentlemen, they'd get us a taxi. And do you know what they did?'

she continued. I was getting rather anxious at this moment. 'Got a supermarket'trolley, bundled us into it and wheeled us home.'

I swear every nerve in my body started to tingle.

'But that's not all,' she went on. 'When we got to the hill by the church, a police car came round the corner – and they ran away.'

I could see it happening. Two flabbergasted policemen cruising past a clattering trolley holding two giggling hysterical teenagers. I went up to my study, wrote it up exactly as it was – but with certain dramatic additions of course – and stored it on disc. It pays to listen to teenagers if you want to write for them.

The sixth thing I ask myself is: *are there any quiet moments when I can reveal greater depth of character and motivation*?

Finally, I ask myself: *has my main character changed in some way by the end of the novel and has she done so in a way which will illustrate my theme*? If the thought and planning I have put into the novel before starting writing was sufficient, I usually find that this factor takes care of itself.

Now I start detailed work on each chapter in turn. I look first for spelling and punctuation errors. For the person whose spelling is weak this can be rather a nightmare – because how can you possibly know if you've made a spelling error if you cannot recognise spelling errors? The only answer is to find a friend who doesn't have that particular educational block and get him or her to read the manuscript armed with a red pen. He may also correct your punctuation at the same time, though frankly, for a teenage novel, this should not prove an insurmountable problem. Your sentences should be simple rather than complex and consequently, apart from quotation and question marks, all you need to master is the knowledge of where to use full stops and commas properly. You may occasionally want to use a semi-colon, but not often.

I also look for needless words. For example, I ask myself: do I need to use 'of course' or 'then' or 'obviously' – to name but a few – where I've used them? If I leave them out, will they be missed? I usually find that not only WON'T they be missed, but the sentences will be IMPROVED.

I look out for adjectives and adverbs I don't need because if I've used strong verbs, then often those adjectives and adverbs which describe or modify the action are superfluous.

Having done all that, I read each chapter aloud, listening carefully for any awkward phrases or sentences. If I find them difficult to read, I simplify them.

This is particularly true of my dialogue. The dialogue is terrible, I may say. So what? I can still improve it. Remembering to keep characters firmly in my mind with the backdrop I have put them against and recalling their reactions to each other, I read the work aloud again. I soon find out what is wrong and then take steps to correct the words I have written. Then I read the dialogue aloud again until I am sure it sounds right.

You will almost certainly find – as I do – that having concentrated on the action and interaction of your characters, the descriptions of the characters and of the locations they find themselves in are weak. You should not have much trouble in rectifying this fault. Try hard to see your character in your mind, having first referred back to your character profiles. Start describing them as vividly and as economically as you can. I like to describe them in action, mingling narrative with dialogue, because it is then they come alive for me.

For instance, instead of writing:

Julia had long fair hair that cascaded down her back and gleamed in the light of the mid-day sun. She was tall and slim, with cream-coloured skin that was almost as smooth as ivory – except that at that moment, two red patches burned angrily on her cheeks.

I prefer to write it like this:

'What do you mean by that?' Julia spun round, her long fair hair, gleaming in the sunlight, cascading in a whirling, turbulent mass down her back.

Karen shrugged her shoulders. 'That's what they're saying about you. That you're stuck-up.'

'That's not true!' Two red patches burned on her cheeks, making her smooth ivory skin seem even paler. 'You know it's not true, Karen.'

Notice that by using dialogue, I've been able to introduce another character and get her reaction as well as Julia's. I've also split up my description of Julia, by interspersing it amongst the dialogue – as and when it became necessary. I described the action of her hair swirling down her back, and then the two red angry patches on her cheeks. The description was in sequence.

I often find at this stage that my descriptions of

locations are not as vividly drawn as they should be. It is usually because I cannot see them clearly in my mind's eye as I'm writing; I'm concentrating on the dialogue and action. If that is the case, and if the location is an imaginary one, I close my eyes and force myself to see it clearly. It usually works. If it is a real location, I pay a brief visit to that location and describe it in words in a small notepad I carry with me – again briefly and as vividly as I can – before I return home. I realise that this may seem tedious or I may be accused of going over the top in my search for reality, but all I can say is: it works and I prefer to do it that way.

Moreover, I look for weak spots in my story – the parts where nothing seems to happen, where there is little conflict. I am not talking about those quiet periods where I can delve deeper into character and motivation. I am referring to those parts which are flat, asking myself how I can improve them. This happened in one of my early novels and I was at a loss to see how I could improve those scenes. Then I remembered some advice I had once been given by a well-published novelist: if your story flags, introduce another character who will create conflict, emotion and suspense.

That first novel was weak in three or four scenes. I recalled what this particular friend had said to me and took his advice. I searched for a character who would do exactly those things – and discovered she was already there. Though in a cursory and inconsequential way; she was there only to give information. I gave her a dynamic part by making her the heroine's rival – for the hero's affections. What else?

It strengthened the story, created much more conflict, emotion and suspense and extended the wordage by almost a thousand words – without having to pad. That was very important.

It is at this stage that I do more research. If, for instance, I have brought into my novel a description of a certain formal scene such as a showjumping competition and I'm not sure about the procedure involved, then I return to a similar event – if it's possible – and observe it with fresh eyes, knowing exactly what I'm looking for. I find that having viewed it as it really is, I can describe it better. If I cannot attend a competition for some reason, then I try to interview someone who is an expert and who can tell me exactly what happens in such a situation. I prefer obviously to visit the actual event, not only because of its immediacy, but because so much more information comes out when you view it.

This was particularly true of one novel which had a motorcycling background. Though I had done my initial research in some detail, nevertheless, when it came to writing the novel, I was not quite sure of the procedure involved during a competition; there were certain things I had forgotten or not recorded.

Luckily, such an event was taking place that weekend, which I attended, knowing exactly what to look for. I watched the actions of spectators as well as competitors; I watched the procedure the motorcyclists had to adopt when they arrived at the forest clearing where this competition was to take place: the judges' tables, the parking places, the routes marked out with tape, the hot-dog vans. Those were things I had not noticed earlier but were important to the creation of authenticity in the story.

I made more copious notes, aware of the pungent odours of decaying vegetation in a forest in autumn – and the equally pungent odours of oil and engine fuel. All those added reality to my final draft.

I examine the ways the characters react to each other and if I have the gut reaction that they are not right, then I think deeply and alter them.

At this stage, I find, as you will, some of my confidence returning; realising what is wrong gives me the impetus and determination to go on to the end of my second draft.

I work chapter by chapter, improving each one, referring to the notes I made during the reading of the first draft and am usually excited by the way it begins to live. The pride of knowing that the second draft is better than the first stirs me on and makes me more determined. I think you'll find the same will happen to you.

When the second draft is finished, I read it once more. This time I search for any anomalies – errors in timing, for instance, where I make sure of the days of the week when something happens and when the action takes place – and correct the manuscript using a red pen. Usually, I find that very little alterations have to be made at this stage; indeed, some chapters may not need revision at all. But if I get once more a gut reaction that something is not quite right, I pay particular attention to that intuitive response. If I feel that way, then the chances are that something really isn't right – I will not be satisfied until I have discovered exactly what it is. I certainly would not dream of sending out the manuscript before I do.

I usually sleep on it; I let my subconscious mind wrestle with the problem even to the extent of pretending not to think about it for a day or two – and usually come up with the solution. When I least expect it.

Finally, I re-read the first chapter and observing some important advice I was once given, I try to make sure that the first sentence is a riveting one, that the first paragraph consolidates that feeling, and that the first page is one which, hopefully, the reader, examining the book

115

in the bookshop, will not want to put down – and end up buying.

Then, and only then, do I submit it to my publisher.

11

WRITING SUCCESSFUL DIALOGUE

And now a few words about dialogue and its functions.
It goes without saying, dialogue is a vital component of
fiction; indeed it could hardly exist without it. And
nowhere is this more true than in teenage fiction. That is
not to say that there is no place for narrative. It is through
narrative that we may get deep inside a character and
provide that emotional depth which is so essential for
reader-identification. Nevertheless, it is dialogue which
makes our stories live and move – and since adolescents
demand action as well as depth of characterisation, it is
necessary to examine the functions of dialogue in order
to be able to write it successfully.

But because we use speech every day, we assume that
speech in fiction is like real-life speech. IT ISN'T. It is
important therefore to be aware that though dialogue in
fiction is not like real-life dialogue, it should sound as
though it is. Real-life dialogue is often tedious. It is full
of hesitations and repetitions. It is often rambling; it
jumps from subject to subject, getting nowhere in particular. Literary dialogue on the other hand must be purpose-
ful, economical and interesting – and create the impression of real speech.

IT IS THE PURPOSE OF THIS CHAPTER TO

EXAMINE LITERARY DIALOGUE AND HELP YOU TO WRITE IT.

First we should examine the two main functions of dialogue:

1. TO DELINEATE CHARACTER, and

2. TO MOVE THE STORY FORWARD.

Let's look at them in more detail. First the delineation of character.

Your dialogue should be tailor-made for the character who is speaking. You should, when you write, hear your characters talk, each in his or her own different way. You should get inside each character, feel what they are feeling, know them and their special speech-patterns intimately. They should become so real that when they 'speak' to you, they will speak in a way that only they can. Indeed, if your dialogue is good, the reader should know exactly which of your characters is speaking even if you haven't specified him or her in your narrative. For example:

'Oh, please . . . please don't ask me. Not again. You know . . . you know I can't come . . . not tonight.'

'Huh! That's what you said last week.'

'I know . . . I'm sorry . . .'

'What's the use of being sorry. This is the third time you've let me down.'

'I . . . I didn't mean to . . .'

'That's what you always say. No. Don't say any more. I've heard enough. You've let me down for the last time. Do you hear? The last time!'

And now this:

'For God's sake! Don't ask me. Not again. You know I can't come. Not tonight.'

'I know . . . but . . . but . . . that's what you said last week.'

'Look. I know what I told you last week. But this is different. Sorry!'

'But what's the use of being sorry. It's all right for you. But what about me? This is the third time you've let me down.'

'So what! Anyone would think I did it deliberately.'

'That's what you always say, isn't it? Always making excuses. No. Don't touch me. You've said enough.'

Can you see how the two situations are basically the same, but the characters different? In the first example, the first character is the weak one, while in the second example, the roles are reversed. But can you see how the characters are revealed? It is through their speech patterns, surely. In the first example, the first character is hesitant, whining, full of self-pity. The converse is true in the second example.

But how do you achieve this difference? The secret is this – please make a note of it – the secret is to know your characters so well that when they speak in your mind, they will speak in character, so that when you write down their words, each will appear as different as chalk from cheese. Assuming, of course, that they are totally different in character.

Let's look at another example of delineation of character through dialogue.

In all the months I'd known him, I don't think I'd ever seen Bob so bitter or angry.

'You really mean it!' he said, his knuckles white as they gripped his coffee mug. 'You really mean it!'

He made me feel terrible. I liked Bob a lot but he was getting too serious lately – and much too possessive as well. I just wasn't ready for it.

'Please . . . please, Bob!' I gulped hard, trying to hold back the tears that threatened to stream down my cheeks. 'It's best this way. Really it is. I don't want to hurt you, but . . .'

He didn't give me a chance to finish. 'Bloody Hell! Would you believe it?' He ran his fingers through his thick dark hair. 'Would you bloody believe it? We've been going steady for almost a year and suddenly she tells me it's all off. And she says she doesn't want to hurt me!'

'Oh, Bob! I don't. I really don't,' I protested weakly. 'We can still be friends.'

There was anger and incredulity in his eyes as he glared at me. 'Friends? You want us to be friends? After this? Not on your bloody life!'

In this extract, we have narrative which complements the dialogue and gives the passage depth. However, the narrative in no way absolves the dialogue from being in character. I think that without the narrative, the dialogue of each character would come over as being distinctive. And that is how it should be. Bob is so obviously angry and disappointed and it shows in the way he speaks; Julie is embarrassed and wishes to avoid the inevitable confrontation – and that too comes over in the way she speaks.

But as I said earlier, it is important that the writer hears those characters speak in his mind before he begins writing. He must get inside both and know how they are feeling before he can write effectively. In other words, the writer must be an actor as well, the stage being his mind. He must write with a small television screen in that area of his head just above his eyes, so that he can 'see' as well as hear his characters. Master that art and a writer's life can be exciting.

Now let's look at the second function of dialogue, which is to move the story forward. In order to do this, it must be logical as well as simple, economical, interesting and effective.

Look at the following example:

I read Andrea's letter a second time. If only I had the courage to join her. But I couldn't leave Dad and Robin. They'd never be able to fend for themselves. Or would they?

On impulse, I phoned Andrea that night. 'Of course you can share the flat with me,' she replied. 'It'll be great to be together again. But Julie. What about your dad?'

'I don't suppose he'll mind,' I said, wishing she hadn't asked. 'Of course I'll have to talk to him first.'

It was suppertime on Friday evening when I finally summoned up enough confidence.

'Dad!' I said nervously. 'Could I . . . could I ask you something?'

He glanced up. 'Of course you can. There's nothing wrong, is there?'

I smiled weakly. 'No. There's nothing wrong.' I hesitated; and then blurted it out – bluntly – not the way I'd intended.

Dad was silent. Robin stopped in the act of taking a large bite of cake and looked at me with large incredulous eyes.

'Going away!' he spluttered. 'To London? But what about us?'

'Be quiet, Robin!' For a few moments, he sipped his tea thoughtfully. 'I think you're right. You're only young once and it's only fair you should have a life of your own.'

121

From this short extract, you will be aware of the turmoil in Julie's mind, her desire for a life of her own struggling against guilt feelings at deserting her father and brother. But more than anything, there is that irrevocable movement towards her leaving the family home, so that the next section must be her departure. The dialogue moves the story forward, at the same time revealing the conflict – internal as well as external – which is at the heart of story-telling.

There are four other functions of dialogue which we ought to consider:

3. TO CREATE CONFLICT, TENSION AND SUSPENSE.

Here is an extract from one of my own novels for teenagers.

I was drying my hands under the hot-air dryer when Sharon came in. She walked right up and in front of the others, prodded me with her fingers. Her nails jabbed into my flesh.

'Just you keep away from Jago,' she said coldly. 'Or else.'

I looked at her in amazement. 'What are you talking about?'

She stood with her hands on her hips, head held to one side, and a sneer on her lips. 'Don't come the innocent with me. You know what I'm talking about. I've just watched the way you were dancing with him. Couldn't get close enough, could you?'

I couldn't believe it was happening. 'You must be mad,' I said, pushing past her.

But she grabbed my arm and swung me round. Her eyes were hard. 'Oh no I'm not. I've noticed the way you've been looking at him. I'm not stupid.'

I was suddenly aware that the others in the cloakroom were watching with amusement.

'Look here, Sharon. Let's get one thing clear. As far as I'm concerned, you're welcome to Jago. I don't want anything to do with him – I don't even like him.'

But even as I said it, I knew it wasn't true. He certainly disturbed me. But deep down he excited me too.

In this passage, I'm sure you'll agree that the conflict inherent in the thrust and parry of the dialogue creates tension, while her thoughts at the end create a feeling of suspense because putting them at the end of the chapter gives them greater significance; we now know that the conflict is far from over.

Here is another example of how dialogue can create suspense. In it, we use the 'cliff-hanger' to do so – and to make the reader want to go on reading.

Jane and Helen were sitting at a small table at the far end of the long room waiting for Colin to return from the bar. Jane tapped her feet to the rhythm of the music, revelling in the flashing lights from the disco, while Helen held her almost empty glass of lager to her lips.

Then her eyes strayed to the entrance where a small cluster of guys gathered. And then she gave a gasp. 'Oh, no!'

'What is it?' asked Jane, a frown on her forehead. 'You look as though you've seen a ghost.'

Helen leaned forward. 'Don't look now,' she said. 'But here comes trouble.'

Before we discuss the suspense aspect of this passage, will you read it again and decide what parts create the suspense. I think you will agree that first comes the gasp, 'Oh, no!' Then there is Jane's remark: 'You look as though you've seen a ghost.' And finally, creating the cliff-hanger, Helen's words: 'Don't look now. But here comes trouble!'

Can you now tell me how suspense is achieved?

I think it is obvious. Suspense in the cliff-hanger situation is achieved by WITHHOLDING vital information from the reader; in this case, the identity of the guy Helen has seen at the door and of course, the reason for the potential trouble. So now you know what you have to do, don't you? Withhold that vital piece of information.

4. TO TELL WHAT HAS HAPPENED 'OFF-STAGE' OR IN THE PAST.

Half an hour later, Erica was still in a deep state of distress. Her mother had made her drink a large glass of brandy but even so, her whole body still shook as she remembered what had just happened.

'Now tell me exactly what happened,' her mother said, sitting at her side and taking her hand in hers. 'Now take your time.'

Erica gulped hard. 'I was on my way home . . . from work . . . Jack had asked me to stay on an extra hour . . .'

'You missed your bus, I suppose.'

Erica nodded. 'Jack offered me a lift, but he lives on the other side of town . . . Anyway . . .'

'You decided to walk instead.'

'That's right. It was a fine evening . . . I thought the walk would do me good.'

She broke down, crying silently into the handkerchief that the sergeant offered her.

'Go on,' he said gently when she had recovered. 'You said you walked over the common . . .'

'That's right. It was light when I started . . . well, just . . . but before I was halfway across . . .'

'Was that when you saw the man?'

She shook her head. 'No that was later . . . when I entered the lane that leads to the railway station. . . .'

'I see. And where was he?'

'Standing under the lamppost at the end . . .'

'The station end?'

'That's right. I remember looking down to avoid some puddles and when I looked up, he wasn't there any more.'

The information could have been given in narrative form; a simple statement of what had happened to Erica as she walked home that fateful evening. However, I feel that in giving the information through dialogue, the emotional aspect is emphasised so that the reader, herself, is involved – and as I've stated before, reader-identification is important. Notice that the information is not given in one large chunk of dialogue; it is dragged out of Erica, which is what would have happened in real life and so authenticity is achieved as well as emotional impact – while the interplay of the two characters alleviates the boredom which would have ensued if only Erica had spoken.

5. TO SHOW EMOTION.

This is really an extension of the above function where the emphasis is placed not on telling what has happened in the past, but rather on the way dialogue can create and heighten emotion in a story. Here are two examples. I'd like you to read both and decide which is the more dramatic and emotional.

I was very nervous the night I went home and told my parents I was pregnant. Mum started to cry and my dad went as white as a sheet. Then he rose from his chair and hit me and I went sprawling into the corner of the living room.

125

Now this:

My parents couldn't believe their ears when I told them.
Mum sat with her cup of tea halfway to her lips and dad let
his evening newspaper fall to the floor.

'You're what?' His words cut me like a whiplash.

My voice was barely a whisper. I couldn't look at him.
'I'm . . . I'm going to have a baby.'

Mum's lips began to tremble and tears came into her eyes.
'Oh no, Gwen. You're not . . .'

There was a hard lump in my throat and my stomach was
a tight knot. 'I'm sorry . . .' My voice quivered and I couldn't
go on.

Dad rose from his armchair and took a few steps towards
me. 'Sorry?' he bellowed. 'Sorry? Is that all you can say for
yourself?'

Blind with rage, he struck me across my face, his hands
big and hard. I went flying across the room and landed in a
heap on the floor.

I don't need ask which is more dynamic. In the first
example, we are told what happened. In the second, by
using narrative as well as dialogue, we not only see what
is happening, but we get the emotion of the situation.
Using action in the narrative and reaction in the dialogue,
emotion is revealed in its most potent form.

6. TO CREATE DRAMATIC IRONY.
In real life we cannot possibly tell what is going on in the
other person's mind; in literature the opposite is true.
The author may give the reader insight into both characters' minds and therefore what they say may have greater
significance than one character realises.

126

Let's look at a situation.

A young seventeen-year-old girl is systematically embezzling from her employer, Mr Carter. The reader knows this from what has happened previously in the story, but Mr Carter does not. He asks her to bank the week's takings for him, imploring her to be careful. Notice her reply.

Mr Carter opened the door of his office and called out to me. 'Jennifer! Come here a minute, will you?'

I glanced at the clock above the door that led into the corridor and gave a low groan. It was ten to five. Ten to five on a Friday afternoon. In half an hour I was due to board the train for a weekend in the West Country with Simon. If Mr Carter made me miss that train!

As I walked into his office, he looked at the shorthand notebook in my hand. 'No need for that,' he said with a smile. 'I just want you to do me a favour, that's all.'

'Oh!' I said warily. 'And what's that?'

He licked the gum on the large envelope he was holding and sealed it. 'Just want you to put this in the night safe in the High Street,' he said. 'The week's takings.'

My heart gave a little flutter. I was almost broke. Paying for my new gear and the pretty nightie I had bought specially for the occasion had robbed me of all my savings.

'Of course you can go straight away,' he went on. 'Susan can manage the rest of the mail. You don't mind, do you?'

Suddenly I made up my mind. I only needed to borrow a few pounds - and only for a few days. I gave him one of my brightest smiles. 'Of course not, Mr Carter. I don't mind at all.'

'Good!' He handed me the packet which must have contained hundreds of pounds. Literally hundreds. 'But do be careful with it,' he added seriously. 'Don't want anything happening to it.'

127

'Don't you worry, Mr Carter,' I replied, walking jauntily
to the door. 'I'll look after it just as though it's my own.'

Can you see the irony of the words? They give the readers
a feeling of omnipotence and also convey the girl's deceit
in a highly dramatic form.

Let us now consider certain other facets.

It is important to vary the length of speeches. After
all, when two people talk, you'll notice that one person
may take a dominant role; he or she may be garrulous
and like the sound of his own voice or on the other hand,
one character may be so annoyed with the other that she
finds it difficult to converse with her partner and resorts
almost to monosyllables.

For example:

'Look, Helen. I really did try to come round last night.
But . . . you know how it is sometimes. I did try, honestly I
did.'

'If you say so.'

'Dianne called round.'

'Huh!'

'I couldn't leave then, could I?'

'Couldn't you?'

'But I'm here now. That's all that matters. So let's go out
somewhere. What about the Troubador?'

'Have you seen my magazine anywhere?'

'Helen. You haven't answered my question.'

'Haven't I? By the way, did you know that Sue's got a
new job?'

'Listen to me, Helen. Please. . . .'

'No. You listen to me. I've had as much as I can take of
your excuses. I know Dianne's your steady but you promised
you'd tell her about us. And have you? Well, have you?'

Notice:

1. Helen's speeches are short. What impressions do they convey?

2. The boy's speeches are far longer. What impressions do they convey?

3. Helen interrupts his speech.

4. Helen gives him a wrong answer to his question 'What about the Troubador?' What impression does that convey?

5. Helen changes the subject. 'By the way, did you know . . .'

6. Then she loses her temper and the truth comes out.

One final word of advice. Don't expect to write perfect dialogue straight off. Not only will you need to practise, but you will also need to edit several times before you are satisfied. Read your dialogue out loud and ask yourself two questions:

Does it sound right?

Is it in character?

Then go ahead and edit again.

12

METHODS OF REVEALING
CHARACTER

And finally, some information on methods of revealing
character, which you may find useful when you write your
novel – together with some exercises. You may use these
exercises before you start writing your novel, while you
are actually writing it or after it has been written and you
are doing the editing.

1. PHYSICAL DESCRIPTION.
This is the simplest but nevertheless an essential way of
delineating character; all novelists use it.

Richard Ellis strode down the mini-thoroughfare, a full six
inches taller than the tallest of the other pedestrians who
jostled along the pavement, his fair wavy hair an untidy
thatch above a broad tanned forehead. He paused mo-
mentarily outside the tall building, gazed up at the legend
above the main entrance, a strange glint in his pale blue
eyes. Then shrugging broad shoulders, he ran up the twelve
steps, three at a time, grim and determined, his jaw firmly
set.

Exercise One

Using a scene from your own novel, describe one of
your characters, preferably one of your main ones, in the
manner depicted above. Try to show YOUR 'PROB-
LEM' CHARACTER IN ACTION.

2. SPEECH.
We also learn much about a character when we are told
how he speaks.

> For a tall man, Webster's voice was unusually high pitched;
> it seemed to warble in the air, tight and hesitant, like a small
> child trying to create music with a reed. And as he spoke,
> his tongue flicked out from time to time, moistening his thin
> lips, accentuating the impression of nervousness.

Exercise Two

Using one of your characters from your novel again – not
necessarily the one described in Exercise One – try to
depict him or her through speech mannerisms.

3. DIALOGUE.
The way in which a character speaks also tells us a great
deal about him. Consider the character we have created
above – Webster. Imagine he is holding a conversation
with another man.

> 'I really must protest, Mr Lavis. Your attitude . . . I must
> say . . .'
>   'What the hell are you twittering on about now, Webster.
> You haven't stopped all morning.'

'I . . . er . . . I mean to say . . . when you consider . . .'
'For Christ's sake, man. Spit it out. Or are you too scared?'

I think you will agree that though there is no description of the characters – no narrative – two quite different people emerge from the way they speak as well as what they say.

Exercise Three

Once again, using two or more characters from your novel, create a sample of dialogue which will show what kind of person each is. You may, if you wish, use some narrative as well.

4. OTHER CHARACTERS' COMMENTS.

We also discover a great deal about characters from what one person says about another.

'But darling! Of course I've heard about Fiona. Who hasn't! I mean . . . for poor Derek to catch her like that . . . with Simon of all people . . . in their own bed. But then I've always said she was a silly little cow. Oh, very pretty, of course. Too pretty for her own good. But then a good figure and long blonde hair isn't everything, is it?'

Notice how we get some physical description as well as an indication of Fiona's foolish promiscuity. We also get some idea of the speaker's vindictiveness – or is it jealousy?

Exercise Four

Using two or more characters from your novel, show them in action in a scene, using the above model as a guide. Try, if you can, to create a subliminal impression of at least one of them, i.e. reveal their characters, not so much through what they say, but rather through what they don't say, particularly in relation to the person they are talking about.

5. HIS OR HER ACTIONS.
Actions tell us a lot about people.

'Look here, Smith.' Robertson grabbed Eric's lapel and thrust his leering face right up against the smaller man's. 'Did anyone tell you what a bloody fool you are?'

Eric stood quite still, ignoring the stench of stale beer on Robertson's breath, and looked up without flinching.

'Takes one to know one,' he said calmly.

Then swiftly and methodically, he brought up one hand, caught hold of Robertson's wrist and twisted it. Less than one second later, Robertson was on the ground, screaming for mercy.

What does that tell us about the two men, I wonder?

Exercise Five

Now try doing the same yourself, but using characters from your own novel instead. Try to create two totally different characters and depict them through their actions as well as dialogue.

6. HIS OR HER REACTIONS TO OTHER PEOPLE AND SITUATIONS.

This too can reveal what a man or woman is really like. Take this situation:

Judd could be brutal with his subordinates when he wished – especially on a Monday morning when the effects of a weekend hangover still lingered.

'Simpkins! Where the hell are you?' He gave a slight shudder and shut his eyes, regretting the way he had shouted. 'Simpkins! Didn't you hear me?'

Simpkins came running from the outer office. 'Yes, Mr Judd.' His voice was breathless with apprehension. 'Did you want something?'

'Did I want something? Simpkins. You're an idiot.'

Simpkins lowered his eyes and looked at the floor. 'Yes, Mr Judd. If you say so.'

And now this:

Judd could be brutal with his subordinates when he wished – especially on a Monday morning when the effects of a weekend hangover still lingered.

'Simpkins! Where the hell are you?' He gave a slight shudder and shut his eyes, regretting the way he had shouted. 'Simpkins! Didn't you hear me?'

Simpkins sauntered from the outer office. 'Yes, Mr Judd!' There was a hint of contempt in his voice which he made no attempt to conceal. 'Did you want something?'

'Did I want something? Simpkins! You're an idiot.'

Simpkins raised his eyes to the ceiling. 'Yes, Mr Judd. If you say so.'

135

Can you see the difference in character between the two men called Simpkins? They are as different as chalk and cheese.

Exercise Six

Using the models above as guides, build up two different scenes using two characters from your novel.

7. HIS OR HER THOUGHTS, I.E. REVERIE.

A very effective method but one which should not be used too often; it can slow down the pace of your novel. Of course that is what you might want to do.

> Robert thought of Pam constantly, ever since she had left home to go to live in a small depressing bedsit in London. It wasn't just that he worried about her; he missed her too. Missed the way she made the house come alive as soon as she entered the front door – an attractive bustling young woman who seemed to laugh and shout and create such havoc that he wondered when it was going to stop. Now it had stopped – and he hated it. He leaned back in the chair, staring blindly at the ceiling, wishing that she was the nine-year-old who rushed to sit on his knee as soon as he arrived home from work. He sighed. That's the trouble when your kids grow up. You don't love them any the less. You just can't show it. At least, not the way you'd like.

Notice how you can get to the thoughts of a man in a way that dialogue can't. Those thoughts are too secret to be spoken aloud, yet they show the warmth of the man.

Exercise Seven

This time, using narrative only, get into the mind of one of your characters and show us what kind of person he or she is.

8. MOTIVATION – GIVE REASONS FOR ACTIONS SO THAT THEY ARE CREDIBLE TO THE READER AND GIVE SOME INSIGHT INTO THE CHARACTER'S REASONS FOR BEHAVING AS HE DOES.

Barlow sat back in his chair, convinced that he had persuaded Wilkinson to invest his money in the project he had taken the last half hour to explain. 'So as you see,' he said rather smugly. 'People need the product more than they realise. And after some high powered advertising, they'll be flocking to buy.'

Wilkinson nodded and pursed his lips. 'Yes. I do believe you're right. Armed with this new device of yours every household in the country will be secure; even the most timid will be able to sleep soundly at night. Yes. Yes,' he went on, a little more eagerly now.

'You've created a piece of equipment that is socially essential given the present high crime rate. I think you can be very proud of yourself.'

Barlow laughed. 'I'm glad you think so, Mr Wilkinson. But I couldn't care less about the social implications. All I'm interested in is making money – as much as I can, as quickly as I can.'

Exercise Eight

Again, using two characters from your own novel, show

them in action in a scene, and reveal through dialogue and narrative, the motives for their actions.

Though the examples given above are geared to the adult market, it should be easy for you to use adolescent characters instead. Practise the skills as often as you can and you will eventually find that you will use them unconsciously when you write.

SO – GO AHEAD AND WRITE.